SCRIBBLINGS

Printed in the United States of America.

ISBN 978-0-9970242-7-2

J Winthrop, Charleston, South Carolina

www.winthropfamily.org

DEDICATION

To my four sons – Jay, Gren, Bayard and Teddy –
all of whom have enriched my life enormously.

TABLE OF CONTENTS

MOSTLY ON
THE ENVIRONMENT

BARRON'S

National Business and Financial Weekly Issue of September 20, 1971

Memo to the Desk-Bound:
Try Running a Tree Farm

Numismatists, art collectors and antique buffs can marshal persuasive facts for making more than a hobby of these fields. Indeed, a good case can be made for going beyond stocks and bonds to establish a foothold in another investment medium. In an age of inflation, the investor's aim is to preserve his buying power – to secure something of lasting value and of limited supply.

Armchair Ecology

The investor who accepts the notion that at least part of his assets should be committed to another area is likely to enjoy psychological benefits as well. Consider the man who develops an interest in land and trees. Here is a ready-made activity for the armchair ecologist. By planting and growing trees, he provides shelter for wildlife, prevents soil erosion, reduces noise pollution, generates oxygen, enriches the soil, and creates a resource the country is likely to need for some time to come. Moreover, an absentee landowner will find trees a crop which, under most circumstances, will grow in value and beauty with each passing year.

Ten years ago, a young man who knew little about real estate and less about trees found some land for sale in South

Carolina. Unable to finance the purchase of a small plantation alone, he was fortunate in finding kindred spirits who shared the cost and gave him a free hand in management. Approximately 1,000 acres were purchased for slightly less than $100,000. (In 1945, land in the region sold for an average of $15 per acre.)

Nearly 200 acres of unhealthy pine trees were partially submerged in swampy land. An additional 200 acres were neither planted in pine nor set aside for crops. The remaining acreage was in fields, and naturally-seeded forest; some small trees had been planted in the fields. Most of the standing timber was slash pine – one of the fastest growing trees in North America. Reaching full maturity in 100 years, the slash pine attains a respectable height of 45 feet with a diameter of six inches in 20 to 50 years. This species of pine grows well in the sandy soil of the Deep South, so it was the obvious principal crop for the property.

The new owners, as noted, found that 40% of their land was under-utilized. Mature trees were cut to provide funds to dig a ditch which, in turn, drained the swampy area. After the bills were paid for drainage and taxes on the land, the surplus was invested in a few saplings, barely a foot tall. They were planted six feet apart, in rows six feet wide.

The open fields were rented to neighboring farmers. The whole plantation was leased to responsible people during the hunting season. Deer, quail and dove are quite plentiful on such property, providing the owners observe basic conservation guidelines. With these two sources of income generating four times the tax requirements, a long-term plan was developed.

It was decided that the venture would be held in corporate form. Long-term capital gains, tempered by a desire to enjoy the land, were the management objective. Any expenses would be paid from cash flow, while the surplus of income over expenses would be reinvested in trees or in clearing the land for seedlings.

Natural Enemies

Soon after the property was acquired, a timber expert visited it to provide professional guidance. He gave his blessing to the basic plan and began educating the owners. He pointed out that the two great enemies of slash pine are red heart rot and fire. While there is no real protection for red rot, definite precautions can be taken against the fire hazard. After the young saplings become five years old, the underbrush should be cleaned out carefully with fire. At this age, the trees – at a height of 8 to 10 feet – will be strong enough to survive the fire. Each subsequent year, burning should be done. However, fire lines at least 20 feet wide should be cut so that no more than 50 acres of trees would be in jeopardy in the event of an accidental fire. (It should be noted that many trees are not fire resistant and burning is not practiced in many other parts of the country.)

The critical period in the slash pine's life is the first year after planting. Lack of sufficient rainfall can create real trouble for the seedlings. The Southern tree farmer must carefully check his crop after the first year of planting and, if the mortality ratio exceeds 20%, the crop should be plowed up and started over again the following year.

Soil should always be tested. The best soil should be kept as open fields, free for the cultivation of other farm crops; trees can be planted in the poorer soil. In addition to providing a source of steady income, the open fields will enhance the property by giving it variety. The hunting rights will have more value, too.

Progress should be reviewed by an expert every five years. Cutting can be done selectively every decade. (Raw harvesting is widely considered to provide the landowner with a higher yield, but the property is decimated by this process and many of the intangible rewards of owning the land will vanish.) Following these guidelines, the value of the timber alone can rise in excess of 8% a year.

The plantation has shown a profit on a cash basis for each of the past 10 years. Since trees have been planted every year, today there are at least 200,000 additional ones on the property. Some $25,000 worth of standing timber has been selectively cut and sold. The owners have developed a worthwhile hobby, experienced a generous share of satisfaction as the property has been developed, and last, but not least, increased their net worth on paper.

Colorado Blues

Acreage in Maine and elsewhere is available today for prices paid 10 years ago in South Carolina. Admittedly, the growing season is shorter, but the same principles can be made to apply. The desk-bound executive can become a Christmas tree farmer without major strain or a steep outlay. The Colorado blue spruce, for example, is one of the best landscaping and Christmas trees on the market. It is a native of the Rocky Mountains and tolerates a remarkable range of growing conditions. These trees should be planted as seedlings after the frost thaws, but before the buds bloom. However, "Colorado Blues" have some odd characteristics. When planted together with Douglas Firs, an aphid frequently passes back and forth between them, causing considerable damage.

Maine is among a number of states offering encouragement to those willing to put land into trees. The cost of planting is minimal and professional advice is willingly provided by the State Forester at no cost to the landowner. A variety of informative brochures are also available upon request.

Once again, the economics are appealing. In addition to the upward trend in land values, the Christmas tree farmer can reasonably expect an 8% - 10% yearly return on his investment. Unfortunately, the rental and hunting rights arrangements are not always easy to develop, but the same approach to the business is as valid in Maine or other states as it is in South Carolina.

Every effort should be made to meet current operating expenses through some sort of annual income not directly related to the trees. If farming and hunting rights cannot be developed, perhaps camping or trailer sites can be created.

The economies of the farming are uncomplicated. With perseverance and a small quota of luck, this type of investment can be most rewarding to the man who likes to take his eyes off the ticker-tape from time to time.

- JOHN WINTHROP

—American Forests—

date unknown

One Man's Woodlands

How a Wall Streeter learned the joys – and profits – of diversification and multiple use on his own tract of land

Those of us who work on Wall Street rarely have time to be philosophical. But if we broaden our horizons just a bit and think of our mission as one of managing assets, we can then write about the joy of growing trees on office time. Growing trees makes sense as an investment. But more importantly, it helps the environment and it enriches our lives.

About 15 years ago, upon my graduating from business school and anxious to conduct an experiment in land management, my father, my brother, and I purchased a small land-investment company in South Carolina. Its property is located in the upper coastal plain, approximately 100 miles inland up the Savannah River. Our purchase consisted of a 1,350-acre tract of land which was approximately half open and half timberland. Our first management objective was developed with great fervor – to maximize the tree production (and presumably the profits) per acre. The trees we selected to plant were mostly slash pine.

Many trees were planted during the first two years, some 108,000 of them over 120 acres of land. Some of the areas were clear-cut and watermelons were planted to condition the soil so that more trees could be planted in the future. Since those first two years, we have planted an additional 316 acres (with approximately

392,400 trees). The trees cost only a few pennies each, but land-clearance costs have increased from roughly $40 per acre 15 years ago to $60 today.

Our land required drainage. Originally, we dug two ditches roughly 1.5 miles in total length. However, it gradually became evident that we needed more drainage. In 1974, through the help of our consultant we designed and dug an additional 1.75 miles

By John Winthrop

Photos by John & Bayard Winthrop

of ditches. This action has alleviated the overall drainage problem and has given us excellent accessibility to some remote areas. The work cost us in the neighborhood of $10,000, but these substantial costs are being more than recovered through harvesting previously inaccessible slash pine.

It was fortunate one day, while we were talking with a friend about our management objectives, he questioned our basic action.

"Do you really want a 1,350-acre tree farm?" he asked. "Nothing but trees?"

We thought about that for a moment. It was suggested that we break up the landscape – a few open fields, maybe some ponds.

This prefab hunting cabin not only increases the value of the land but also allows builder to modify the design to suit the surroundings.

Though no decision was made immediately, we continued to ponder the idea seriously. The economic side of the question was simple. Expenses were bound to trend upward. Even in the early 1960s it was obvious that inflation was the most conspicuous fact of economic life. From the outset we had hoped that the demand for trees would give us a comfortable margin of safety in keeping our revenues ahead of our expenses. Now, if some land was to be diverted from trees to open fields and man-made ponds, other sources of revenue might be developed. As manager of assets, I saw much sense in the wisdom of diversification.

Our management plan changed. We developed a more aggressive attitude toward getting a respectable flow of income from the farming rights. Twenty percent of the land was left open as the farmland was identified.

Our main crops, aside from trees, have become corn and soybeans. It is agreed that as the crops are planted each year, the farmer will continue to build our agricultural land through sound fertilization, weed control and good farming practices. Rent on farmland has risen from $7 to $18 per acre per year over the past decade.

Hunting rights were considered as another source of revenue. The area has abundant deer, quail, doves and ducks. Through a close friend, we found a group of responsible hunters who appreciated the conservation of our natural resources. For the most part, our hunters came from nearby communities.

In order to make sure that conditions would remain favorable for the variety of wildlife indigenous to South Carolina, one of our first projects was to prescribe-burn. This practice helped develop food and shelter for wildlife, principally deer and quail. The hunters assumed responsibility for any further development of food and shelter. At the same time they paid us a dollar an acre for the area hunted, an amount sufficient to cover the real-estate taxes.

Our property now has two ponds that we built. They are fed through natural springs and one of the principal drainage ditches. The first pond covers approximately 10 acres, the second about 30. The good water source and available foods for fish enabled us to stock the ponds with bream and bass; we realized that in a short period of time, fishing would be very respectable. Our fourth source of income was realized through leasing the fishing rights.

Finally, a log cabin completed the picture. Prefab log cabins can be built at reasonable cost. They can also be redesigned, if ready-made plans appear to lack imagination. A living structure with few original modifications provided a fifth source of income. The log cabin was constructed on the edge of the larger pond.

A new multiple-use management plan was put in place. Though new profit centers were created, tree farming remained the basic foundation of the enterprise. The business-school approach prevailed in the management of the property. To maximize profits within a stable framework of diversification – that is now our goal.

Favored by a long growing season, the trees flourished. The demand for agricultural goods made the decision to go into farming a wise one. Conservation-minded hunters were found. The fish grew faster than the revenues from fisherman, but the effort clearly made sense. Finding a tenant for the log cabin was the final accomplishment. We got our whole act together.

The most rewarding aspect of the entire experience has been the intangible dividends. As a landowner/timber farmer, I have been able to introduce my three sons – John, Jr., Grenville, and Bayard – to the joys of growing

trees and the satisfaction of developing such a place over a period of time.

The hunting, fishing, and canoeing have provided us with a first-class recreational retreat. Some of our happiest moments together have been spent in the cabin we designed together. Planning for the future we occasionally have conflicting ideas now that the boys are reaching their teen years.

A unique dimension of the property has been the discovery of ancient artifacts of American Indians on the property. Projectile points and pottery have been found in certain areas, and some items have been

The author's son Bayard displays the result of his battle of wits with a gray squirrel.

carbon-tested. Bayard, my youngest son, has taken a particular interest in this aspect of the property; at the early age of seven and eight he discovered several artifacts of consequence. The Peabody Museum of Harvard University did some serious research on the artifacts and reported that many of them dated back thousands of years before Christ. Some were actually as old as the pyramids of Egypt, and the pottery is judged to be among the oldest found anywhere in North America.

It has been over this past year that we have become interested in the idea of developing a wildlife sanctuary on the property. Our intentions are to take an area around one of

LEFT: To make sure conditions on the property would favor indigenous wildlife, spring burning of slash pine was undertaken.

BELOW: Stocking the man-made ponds with bass and bream has increased the recreational value of the land and also the source of income through leasing of fishing rights.

the ponds of approximately 50 acres and prohibit hunting.

Conditions on the entire property are ideal for birds. The trees, while cleansing the air and offering protection to the soil, also offer shelter and a home for many different species of birds and a resting place for deer and other wildlife. With potential revenues of more than $100,000 coming from timber operations over the next 15 years, the trees remain the key to the success of the venture.

The evolution in the management objective has been an interesting experience worth sharing. The place has become much more than just a tree farm. Most importantly, we have now learned that sound management and environmental protection are not mutually exclusive. Indeed, one reinforces the other over the long term.

John Winthrop is Chairman of Wood, Struthers & Winthrop Management Corp. in New York City. A director of the Fresh Air Fund and the National Audubon Society, he has had articles published in numerous journals.

THE
GREENWICH
REVIEW

November 1978

The Black Mulberry Project

Nearly 350 years ago, John Winthrop sailed from England with a company of 900 persons to assume his duties as first elected governor of the Massachusetts Bay Colony. For the rest of his life he remained a leader in formulating that earliest American colony's principles and implementing its policies, and as such helped set standards for much of the English New World. Another link in the same chain between old and new, these centuries later, has recently been forged – appropriately, an environmental one. Seeds from the ancient black mulberry tree under which John Winthrop and his companions gathered to plan the Bay Colony voyage have been for the first time successfully raised in the New World – by a descendant and namesake of that seventeenth century governor.

The black mulberry tree which grew in the courtyard of the family manor in Groton, England never had much meaning to me when I read about it in books. It was an ancient tree — still standing long after the house itself had crumbled—bearing fruit only occasionally and providing a curiosity for tourists.

A visit to Groton just a few years ago changed my feeling about that tree quite fundamentally. The pilgrimage was planned so that I could participate in a ceremony of dedication for a restored portion of the ancient chapel. Ties with the Winthrop family had been maintained over three hundred years; I felt honored to be invited for the occasion.

Having nearly forgotten about the old tree, I was surprised to see that it had been made into a historic shrine. The British seem to care more about their trees and perhaps even more about their history than we do.

Mary Gates, who welcomed me to Groton, introduced me to the famous black mulberry. On a foggy, damp afternoon, we tramped across a meadow to examine the solitary tree. A few green leaves graced its gnarled trunk and branches, and miraculously, as if in honor of the anniversary, some berries had appeared— the first, I was told, in five years.

No one seemed to know exactly how old the tree was. Certainly no one in the community whom I asked at a welcoming party that afternoon could tell me, but it was the consensus that the tree could not live much longer. Some even felt that the fruit borne by the famous tree might not be seen another year.

At some point on that memorable afternoon, it occurred to me that this tree should have progeny on American earth. Just as the hardy citizens of Groton set sail for the New England shores in the early 1600s to populate the New World, so should this black mulberry tree now have a link to America of its own.

Mary Gates seemed enthusiastic about the project as well. Together we collected berries on the ground and placed them in a plastic bag, resolving to launch an experiment of minor historic consequence.

Within a week, I had arrived in New York and transported the valuable plastic bag to the headquarters of the National Audubon Society. A member of the staff helped me initiate the freezing and planting. For a six-month period, we worked on the seeds—simulating the natural conditions which make the seeds germinate after passing through the digestive tract of a bird.

Sadly, this first effort failed. Nothing happened. Apparently the seeds had become mildewed on the voyage back to the U.S. Meanwhile, however, I had described the project to John Andresen, Ph.D., member of the board of the National Audubon Society and a well known professor and tree expert. He became interested in the experiment and agreed to drop by Groton and meet with Mary Gates the following year in hopes of getting some additional seeds.

Within a year, we had received the happy news through Mary that the famous tree had borne fruit for the second consecutive

Sam La Face and John Winthrop (left to right) survey the mulberries' progress at the end of their first summer on John Street. Sam, quite familiar with the trees' background and native environment for the seedlings in their Connecticut home, as well as for other species of trees such as the eight-year-old blue spruce in the background which John Winthrop raises on this sheltered, east-facing hillside. Many of these trees have been donated to local organizations and town improvement projects. The young mulberries, a special care, having graduated from their earliest protective wire fencing, will be shielded from their first New England winter with foliage, salt hay and tenting then transplanted elsewhere in the spring.

year, and John Andresen returned to the University of Toronto with another collection of seeds—enough, in fact, to give me a few which I attempted to process once again, but this time under the guidance of an expert.

Dutifully, I mixed the seeds with sand, froze them during the winter months—November through March— and then separated them into boxes, watering them twice a week after burying them as instructed a quarter of an inch in the soil, one inch apart from one another. Again nothing happened. No magic green sprout appeared as the April weeks drifted by. But, Dr. Andresen was more successful. Triumphantly, he announced that he had produced eighteen black mulberry seedlings in Toronto. After a year of growing, he would transport them south across the border into Connecticut where I lived.

All went well during the ensuing year. The following April the trees were a year old and the root structure had developed in healthy fashion. Before leaving for an Audubon board meeting, John Andresen packed ten in a bag and came to spend a weekend at my Greenwich home. Together with my sons, we planted the trees in April 1978.

As I write this report, the trees appear healthy. All ten have sported bright green leaves, and are protected from hungry deer by chicken wire. Ahead of us lies the pleasure of distributing these trees among interested people and societies in America. Recently, we have learned that very few, if any, black mulberry trees have found their way to America. After attempting to midwife the birth of the species myself, I can appreciate why black mulberries found the voyage to be an even more difficult one than our ancestors did.

date unknown

Plenty of good reasons for planting a single tree

The world is running out of trees. Thousands of acres of forest are being destroyed every day by mankind to make way for the needs of "civilization."

Additional acres are destroyed by fire, by disease, or by natural causes. In addition to replacing those trees that are gone, there are many good reasons to plant a tree or many trees, for those who have the opportunity Among them:

• They beautify the landscape. Think how our living space would look with no trees at all.

• Trees purify the air. In fact, they provide oxygen for us to breathe.

• They prevent soil erosion. On slopes, trees contain soil by their root structure.

• They prevent wind erosion. Planted in strips they can dull the effect of high winds which rob the land of badly needed topsoil.

• They enrich the soil. The organic addition to the soil a tree provides improves the quality of the earth.

• They provide mankind a vital resource. Beyond firewood and building material, trees provide a wide variety of additional byproducts today which improve the quality of life.

• Trees provide jobs. Both directly and indirectly, timber and wood products help the employment statistics.

Most importantly, the satisfaction gained from planting a tree is immeasurable. Trees planted in early, or even mid-life, can provide the opportunity to transform the landscape. What could be more important! It can make us feel better even though trees planted now are likely to outlive all of us.

Mr. Winthrop is a Greenwich resident and a member of the National Audubon Society. He is president of his own investment management company, John Winthrop & Co. in New York. He also grows trees in South Carolina.

Greenwich Time

Thursday, October 14, 1982

The need for an environmental dialogue

National Audubon has developed a list of major criticisms of Secretary Watt's work in the Interior Department and of the Reagan administration's environmental policies. The accusations are broadcasted widely and include the following:

1. Wilderness Areas – The administration has tried to open federally protected wilderness to oil and gas drilling.

2. National Forests – Planned over-cutting will destroy virgin stands and wildlife.

3. National Parks and Wildlife Refuges – Authorized land acquisition has been delayed and responsibility for urban parks has been abdicated.

4. Wildlife – The attempt to lift the ban on Compound 1080 on public lands will kill coyotes and threaten other creatures.

5. Endangered Species – The budget for protecting endangered species has been cut severely; no new species have been added to the list for protection.

6. Clean Air – Clean air quality standards have been reduced and enforcement has slacked.

7. Acid Rain – The administration appears to be oblivious to the hazards of acid rain on all life.

8. Energy – There has been no vigorous pursuit of alternative energy development which would benefit all forms of life.

9. Strip Mining – Enforcement is almost non-existent; the staffs of the Office of Surface Mining have been cut by nearly 70 percent.

10. Demographics – There is far too little sense of urgency over the need to control population growth within the U. S. and worldwide.

The Secretary of the Interior, Mr. James Watt, on the other hand, considers himself an environmentalist. He obviously has a burning sense of mission. Included among the list of accomplishments by the Department of the Interior are the following:

1. Approval has been given to the apportionment of $107 million in federal aid to all 50 states plus Puerto Rico, Guam, American Samoa, the Virgin Islands and the Northern Marianas for sport fishing

29

and wildlife restoration and hunter safety programs.

2. The Office of Surface Mining launched a joint federal-state program to crack down on wildcat coal operations in Eastern Kentucky and Tennessee.

3. An inventory of free flowing streams and rivers has been produced for the first time – some 1,500 stream segments totally 61,700 miles.

4. The golden access passport has been created to enable the physically disabled and blind to obtain free entry to national parks and recreation areas.

5. Secretary Watt has called for an inventory and orderly development of America's natural resources set aside for multiple use to avoid a crisis situation where natural resources might be developed without regard to environmental considerations.

6. Greater protection has been given to the humpback whale in their swimming ground in Glacier Bay, Alaska; the California condor's recovery plan has received Secretary Watt's full support as well.

7. Great emphasis has been put on bringing existing parks up to acceptable standards for safety and health.

8. Ducks, geese, and migratory birds have been helped by the acquisition and funding of wetlands.

9. Secretary Watt has initiated a program requiring concessionaires at Yellowstone and Denali National Parks to contribute a significant share of their earnings to permit improvements for visitors.

10. Endangered and protected American reptiles have benefited from a sweeping series of arrests by the agents of the Fish and Wildlife Service.

The ten accusations and ten accomplishments are not all-inclusive. Nor are they as elaborate nor as documented as either side would have them. But they do give a fairly clear idea of the broad gulf which separates the environmentalists from the administration these days.

Sadly there is no winner. The staff of the National Audubon Society and similar leading conservation organizations could embark on a useful dialogue with their counterparts in government, but communication has ground to a halt as the acrimony has mounted.

There is a case that can be made for changing methods. The shrill screaming may be less effective than quiet, polite debate. An effort to add knowledge and support for a change of direction is worth a shot.

John Winthrop is a Greenwich Resident.

Greenwich Time

date unknown

Trees are the timber of this community

Driving through the back country of Greenwich – particularly during this time of year – one finds it difficult to believe that without much traffic it is possible to drive to Times Square in an hour. A bounding deer or the glimpse of a squirrel or a rabbit or the sound of songbirds or the smell of the springtime flowers combine to create this unusual slice of very elegant suburbia.

But most of all, we are blessed with trees – many trees of different species and shapes, shrubs and tall trees, hardwoods and softwoods, evergreens, fruit-bearing trees, flowering trees and budding trees. It's a good time to pause and consider all the splendid things trees do for us, for our total environment and for the quality of our lives.

There are many here and elsewhere who make their living growing trees. It's not a bad business, with the demand for paper, for housing, for landscaping and for timber production of all kinds. With the irresponsible cutting of trees, the elimination of forests, in fact, around the world, it can be said that we represent the Mideast of timber.

One can easily identify industries that have developed around wood and paper products. In the southeastern United States, it is impossible to sit in the middle of many of those small sleepy towns for a morning without seeing railroad cars or trucks carrying loblolly sawtimber logs going through town on the way to the nearest sawmill on any given day.

Here in Greenwich, landscaping and shrubbery activity is very much in evidence. Indeed, the revenues generated from the tree business in its many forms have been and will continue to be formidable – particularly in the eastern United States.

Beyond all the economic benefits of trees, however, pause to consider all of the additional benefits. One doesn't have to be an outspoken environmentalist to notice among other things …

• Trees beautify the landscape from Maine to Florida and westward to the stately redwoods of Washington and the coast. The vibrant green of the budding leaves at this time of year almost symbolize revival and hope.

• Trees provide for wildlife. Imagine our lives without all the birds and creatures that make their homes among the trees. In a very real sense, trees conserve, protect and shelter all woodland birds and creatures.

• Trees conserve the soil. They have protected the soil against water and wind erosion. In some cases, they retard the process; in still others, they prevent it.

• Trees purify the air. The cleansing process of the trees around us is something we too often take for granted.

It appears that building can never stop in a community as vital or dynamic as ours. But building requires almost always the destruction or removal of trees. Too often, trees are removed without any thought being given to replacement.

Trees planted by some of us this year may not – indeed should not – be harvested or cut in our lifetimes. But surely they will improve the quality of life for those who follow us ... and the world will be a better place.

John Winthrop, a Greenwich resident, is the founder of John Winthrop & Co., a New York-based trust-management and investment firm. In 1979, he interrupted his career in investment management to work for the Republican Party in a national election campaign. He is a member of the Greenwich Time Board of Contributors.

"Letters to a Son," *publication and date unknown*

Bush plans to clean up pollution

Dear Teddy:

You don't seem to be developing much interest in the race for the presidency between George Bush and Michael Dukakis. Perhaps this is because you are only two years old.

On the other hand, you have already developed a keen interest in the great outdoors. Chasing a ball in an open field, reaching for frogs as they jump into a pond or chasing after a rabbit telling the terrified animal you want to "hold it" are among your favorite sports. A boat ride and a visit to a beach seem to make you as happy as anything you have experienced in your short life so far. So it looks as if you will become one of those people who will care very much about the preservation of our fragile environment – about this beautiful planet where you and your mother and I, along with many millions of other Americans, have the privilege to spend this time together.

At some later date you will appreciate the fact that some of our leaders are beginning to understand how urgent environmental problems are. Last month, George Bush visited Boston. Boston Harbor, which the Massachusetts Water Resources Authority has called the dirtiest harbor in America, has the largest concentration of DDT in the nation. Boys and girls your age living in Roxbury and Dorchester and South Boston can't visit the beaches; sludge is released less than a mile offshore, with one ton of PCBs accumulating in the harbor annually. Recently, work has begun on the harbor, but it has been delayed far too long. This is a particularly meaningful example to me not only because this is very near the place I was born and grew up, but also it is an example of the growing urgency of problems developing across the country and, indeed, around the world.

When he visited Boston Harbor, George H. W. Bush made several points which created for some of us the first hopeful signs that these problems will be addressed in a serious way for the first time. Some examples:

On *acid rain*: The time for study is over; the time for action is upon us. Bush said that he would establish a program of emission reduction on a specific timetable. This will be good news for all Americans and for Canadians who have been reminding us of the problem for years.

On *toxic waste dumps*: The vice president indicated he would strengthen enforcement action against those who dump poison.

On *ocean dumping*: A stronger effort to track disposal of medical wastes and a clear ban on ocean dumping would be recognized priorities in a Bush administration. The

Coast Guard would be given more strength to stop illegal dumping at sea.

On *ozone depletion*: Within a reasonably short period of time a conference would be convened in Washington, with representatives from all nations, to establish way of cooperating on matters relating to ozone depletion and global warming. Deforestation, another global problem, would be the focus of such a gathering as well.

There are additional elements in the Bush agenda on environmental problems, but the main point is that the planning process is underway. This is a good beginning; it deserves our support, because there isn't much time left.

So my hope is that you will go back to enjoying the wonders of nature. The frogs and bunnies are good companions along with other living creatures, although most of them won't let you get very close to them. I'll forgive you for not paying much attention to presidential debates. But I won't be so forgiving of any of our leaders if they ignore these problems; the quality of our life together depends on what action is taken. It looks like candidate Bush is off to a good start.

When I get home, let's take a walk together outdoors.

Love,
Dad

John Winthrop, who maintains homes in Greenwich and South Carolina, is the founder of John Winthrop & Co., a Charleston, SC-based trust-management and investment firm. He has been active in the national Republican Party organization.

MOSTLY ON
FINANCE

Financial Analysts Journal®

September-October 1969

Layman's View of Computer Power

Over the past five years the computer has hit Wall Street with the force of dynamite. To a few it represents a threat to the accustomed way of doing business; to a few it represents an unequalled opportunity to revolutionize our profession; to most of us it represents an intriguing puzzle – a new dimension. The capabilities and limitations of the computer are not well understood.

With so few people understanding the investment business as well as computer technology, most initial steps in the uses of the machines took place in the back offices of brokerage firms. But increasingly, interest has centered on its application as a tool for investment analysis and portfolio management. The growing attendance at seminars and conferences devoted to this subject bear witness to the realization that our work does indeed offer opportunity for a scientific quantitative approach. In the best of all possible worlds one would have thought that the portfolio manager or the security analyst, living in a world of numbers, would have been the first to apply the computer intelligently.

However, if we were to divide applications of the computer into three broad categories: back office administrative work, portfolio management and security analysis, and management decision-making, we could say with some justification that the investment community is now beginning to focus in earnest on the second activity. Game theory – at least at it applies to the actual management of firms – is still beyond reach. What then can the typical asset manager expect in the years ahead? Where is the tide of renewed interest in computer techniques taking the vast majority of serious students of investments – most of whom are totally unschooled in the use of the machines? Let us first look at where we now stand – at what the computer is doing for us.

The Present

Screening techniques are used widely as an efficient method of eliminating companies of marginal interest to the analyst. An illustration of this approach may be useful for any who are unfamiliar with it. Now an analyst can request a print-out from a computer – assuming the appropriate data has been stored – on any company among the 1800 catalogued in Standard & Poor's Compustat service which meet a given set of criteria such as the following: sales in excess of $50 million; one million shares or more outstanding; growth rate in earnings per share exceeding fifteen per cent; and a price-earnings ratio of twenty or less. The time saving advantages of this approach are obvious. Immediately the account manager or analyst can focus on an abbreviated list of companies. Such selectivity should lead to more thorough research on those companies of interest.

In addition, the computer is currently being used as an aid in highlighting the relationship between significant financial measurements of a company. Ratios of particular interest to an analyst can be stored and calculated instantaneously. For example, the historical price-earnings ratio, the return on assets, the capital structure, and the current ratio of several companies can be compared. An industry composite can be prepared for reference purposes. Once again time is saved and the "dog work" is largely eliminated from the analytical process.

The computer has made regression analysis an accessible method of attempting to understand the relationships among various financial variables. A dependent variable, such as a company's earnings, can be measured against a series of independent variables – capital investment, growth of sales, aggregate economic data, etc. … Despite its limitations this process provides a rigorous and sometimes more revealing method of studying the relationships among the various quantifiable characteristics of a company or an industry.

The Future

As we look to the future we can expect the computer to become more fully utilized. This point can be made with certainty since our profession – as conspicuously as any – has merely begun to learn the capabilities (and limitations) of the computer. We can only guess what the new directions will be, but some indications are clearly visible.

Model building and simulation are likely to be employed to a far greater degree than at present. These techniques provide a method of considering a multitude of variables simultaneously – an impossible feat for the human mind. Moreover, analysts will be able to refine their ability to isolate and then examine more closely those variables which are most relevant to a particular company's level of earnings. Those that have worked with model building in the past have discovered the difficulty of quantifying all the significant variables in any environment, but this limitation has not been an insurmountable obstacle. Analysts of the future can be expected to hypothecate different states of nature, different economic conditions, and to ask the intriguing question "what would happen if …" The result: a refined appreciation of what are the most sensitive and most important variables in any particular situation.

The advent of time sharing has already had a fundamental effect on the thinking and the approach of many analysts. The economic feasibility of time sharing assures us that the dialogue between analyst and the computer will become richer and more frequent. But time sharing provides more than the advantage of significantly reduced costs. It also has improved communication between man and machine with the development of nontechnical computer language. First Financial Language (FFL), for example, can be mastered within two or three sessions. Time sharing permits the analyst to interact with the computer, to ask questions, to creatively devise and explore new problems.* In the future, packaged or "canned" systems of various models will be made available so that analysts can broaden their dialogue considerably.

The casual observer needs little exposure to time sharing to grasp its implications for the analyst. Discipline will be required: all inquiries must be carefully formulated; the significance of various inquiries must be weighed and analyzed. But experimentation and innovation will yield results as the analyst becomes comfortable at the terminal and the ease of communication between man and machine is improved.

The availability of time sharing systems of statistical and screening techniques and the use of simulation through model building can potentially lead to more carefully structured analysis. The process of analysis itself is likely to become more carefully scrutinized. To this extent the analyst is likely to become more introspective. The desirable end result will, hopefully, be a more thorough and disciplined process.

Resulting side benefits can be expected – a more standardized approach to accounting procedures, for example. We have seen some of this already, especially in the development of reliable data banks. Less dependence on junior analysts or backup personnel for statistical work may also be expected. Even a refined method of interviewing companies is a logical expectation as these techniques become more widely developed. Analysts at First National City Bank have indicated this to be the case.

Portfolio managers and analysts will be looking into the decision-making process itself more in the years ahead. Very little is known about what actually triggers an investment decision at present. As in case of certain consumer products, we cannot tell if a decision to buy a particular brand is made as a result of advertising, hearsay, or impulse. Many portfolio managers know little about their own decision-making process and even less about their methods of reviewing accounts. Clearly if more progress is made in understanding this mysterious realm, the computer can and will be used as an aid in sharpening the focus of money managers.

A more obvious area where progress can be made – and still a ripe area for drastic reform – is that of keeping a closer account of portfolio managers and of analysts. In the case of account managers their performance must be judged in relationship to the objectives of the accounts. We can expect to see more strenuous efforts to quantify objectives in the future. Likewise, with analysts, their performance, or their recommendations, can be measured against indicators of the industries they follow. These procedures are likely to be used as internal management aids and as a method of rewarding various firms with accounts or commission business.

Summary and Conclusion

An interesting picture emerges for the observer unskilled in the refinements of computers power. The limitations of the computer are very real: the input must be accurate; the database must be complete; questions must be asked carefully; everything must be specified. Implicitly the computer requires some knowledge of math and statistics in order to fully exploit its capabilities. The discipline which the computer demands – superimposed on the discipline already required by our profession – will surely make our work more scientific. It will probably also make our work more rational, more efficient, and more competitive. As many others have said before, however, the computer will never replace the man. Our profession will always remain an art as well as a science, since certain critical variables cannot be effectively quantified or reduced to a yes-no logic.

──Trusts&Estates──

July 1973, The Institutional Investor

Investment Approach – A Case For Quality

The so called "growth stocks" appear to be selling at preposterously high price/earnings multiples, while hundreds of companies on and off the New York Stock Exchange are selling at what appear to be bargain prices. Many sophisticated money managers are calculating book values, salivating over high yields, and considering the probabilities of takeovers and turnarounds. The pursuit of value is a valid and defensible philosophy of investing, particularly at this point in the market. The purpose of this article is to offer the alternative approach – the pursuit of high quality predictable growth – at a time when it may appear to be unrealistic.

Above all, portfolio managers need a philosophy, a discipline and an approach to investing to be effective in their work. The graveyards of bankrupt investment firms and wiped-out speculators are filled with the bones of those who had no rules and were governed by fads and impulses. So we must study our trade; we must learn what forces govern equity and bond prices; we must determine our time span.

Portfolio Time Dimension

The time dimension is important. It must be argued that the professional money manager should be given time to work through all phases of the business cycle before he is tested adequately. He must demonstrate his ability to take a defensive posture in a down market, and he must maximize his gains in an up market. He must assume one posture in the initial stages of a bull market, and another in the advanced stages of a bull market. He must emphasize certain securities in an uncertain market and other securities in a raging bear market. The test comes in orchestrating all these and other steps as the investment environment changes, which in turn implies a three- to five-year period of performance measurement.

Educating the client to look at his portfolio's performance over a five year period, rather than from quarter to quarter, can be difficult, if not impossible. Time is always well spent in cultivating a clear understanding of objectives on both sides. If the long view can be accepted – the five-year approach – a big step has been made in eliminating the pressure to find the fad industry or the odd speculative stock that will double over a six month period.

It then becomes a matter of considering the variables that determine the price actions of stocks and bonds. As we all know, the list is interminable: war and international unrest; inflation and unemployment; monetary and fiscal policy; productivity and profitability; hopes and fears. But the ability to sustain a predictable improvement in earnings potential remains the most important element in establishing equity prices. As for fixed income securities, their prices are governed by the climate of the money markets and the ability of the issuer to meet his obligation.

Money Manager's Real World

Now, let us take a look at the real world of the money manager. For the sake of discussion, let us assume that the annual expenses of an account amount to two per cent of the value of the stocks and bonds under management; charitable gifts, estate planning, and taxes combined amount to another two percent of the portfolio. Finally, the inflationary expectation is four per cent. This means that the money manager must be expected to reach for a total return of at least 8 – 10%. A total return of eight per cent amounts to nothing more than staying even in terms of buying power – the most realistic and meaningful measurement.

If we accept the need to take the long view, and if we accept the premise that earnings improvement is the prime mover in determining equity prices, we can begin to develop a game plan. The predictability of earning imporovement becomes terribly important. When we begin to reach for a total return in the 8-10% range, or above, it becomes obvious that we will need to

focus on those companies superior and sustainable earning power. These quality growth stocks have to become the core holdings of portfolios under management.

Premiums of Core Stocks

Traditionally, such stocks sell at a substantial premium in the market place. Conservatively, we may wish to assume they will sell at less of a premium in the future. For the sake of demonstration, we will make the assumption that they will be able to maintain their growth rate at stated levels, that five equal commitments will be made, and that the shrinkage of the P/E multiples will develop from the purchase to the sale in five years time. (See *Exhibit I* accompanying the text. The calculations therein assume no pay out of dividends – again, a conservative assumption.)

Despite a substantial deterioration of the price/earnings multiple, the rate of appreciation is at a comfortably high average level of 11.8 per cent. This rate will improve further if the stocks are held and the lower price/earnings multiple remains firm. The all-important factor is the reliability of the earnings growth rate. This is a different way of suggesting that quality is important. Perhaps we should dwell a bit more on the various dimensions of this term, which surely mean different things to

			Sale	
		Purchase	(P/E multiple	Compound
	Growth	(Current P/E	after holding	Rate of
Stock	Rate	multiple)	stock 5 yrs.)	appreciation
A	10%	20	16	5%
B	12%	24	20	8%
C	15%	26	21	10%
D	20%	30	24	15%
E	30%	50	35	21%

EXHIBIT I

different people.

Desirable Characteristics of An Investment

The notion of quality in the selection of securities means predictability of performance and implies leadership within a given industry. Those who live by this doctrine are concentrating on stocks of companies with a preponderance of several familiar characteristics:
- innovative management;
- relatively small labor content as a percentage of total costs;
- miminal dependence upon swings in commodity prices;
- industry leadership of identification with a proprietary product;
- global marketing capabilities;
- paucity of environmental problems; and
- strong balance sheet.

All of these elements determine a company's edge on the competition in governing its own destiny. Each must be monitored and scrutinized very carefully. When the environment changes, or when one of the favorable characteristics is altered, the portfolio manager must know it at once, so that he can weigh the importance of any such development.

The approach is equally valid with bonds. The ability of the issuer – be it a corporation, a municipality, or a federal government – to meet its obligation must be measured carefully on a continuing basis. Again the reliability of predictability of the debt coverage must be regarded carefully. The quality rating, of course, will reflect the security of future payments.

The portfolio manager will be accepting a lower payout in his bond portfolio in return for the added security of higher quality bonds. This approach correctly suggests that the bond portfolio will reduce somewhat the total return of the total portfolio as an acceptable price for safety. The bond portfolio will provide a strong defense; the equity portfolio will be structured to provide a strong offense.

Conclusion

Fundamental research is the keystone to the success of this approach. It is suggested that selection of securities is far more important than timing. The chartists will be of limited value, although a good technician can be a helpful guide to any money manager once the fundamental research is done. The computer, particularly as a screening device for measuring growth rates and financial structures of corporations, can be useful as well. But the primary burden falls upon the portfolio manager; he must establish the guidelines while the research analyst monitors corporate developments.

This disciplined, structured approach to the art of managing investments may sound simplistic to some. The search for quality does not exclude the need to recognize value, nor the necessity to study the sources of earnings and the soundness of balance sheets. Neither does the long term view offer any excuse to be reckless in the acquisition of high multiple stocks, nor to avoid all other equities during the various phases of the market. But, combined, intelligently, this method can postpone the need for tranquilizers.

The author is head of the Investment Advisory Department at Wood, Struthers & Winthrop, a New York City investment-brokerage firm. He holds a B.A. from Harvard University and an M.B.A. from Columbia. Previous articles by Mr. Winthrop have appeared in the Financial Analysts Journal *and* Barron's.

PENSI⬤N WORLD

September 1976

A stock selection yardstick:
Check the track record

There has always been a "big winner" stock or industry in any given year. But how many of them have performed consistently well, year after year? Portfolio management, writes John Winthrop, chairman of the investment firm of Wood, Struthers & Winthrop Management Corp., should not be an exercise in technical gymnastics. Rather, it should be based upon looking at the facts and figures – inside and out, prudent judgment – and a sense of history.

A sense of history is valuable in most fields of human endeavor. As our country celebrates its 200th anniversary, thoughtful Americans will pause to consider the positive and reinforcing elements that have made our experiment in democracy work. At the same time, some of our mistakes may be studied.

Although it is difficult to verify and impossible to measure, one might argue that we are in the middle of a shift to the right in our political history precisely because of our collective sense of what has happened. We seem to be looking inward and we seem to be shying away from involvement overseas. We seem to be leaning toward fiscal orthodoxy, toward balanced budgets, toward sterner disciplines. In our view, some of these trends are encouraging and worthy of our attention as investment managers.

It is just possible that we have learned something from our involvement in Viet Nam and our Watergate agony, the oil embargo and the mismanagement of our urban centers. Whatever the case, it seems clear that there is value in developing a clearer understanding of all the steps which lead to each of the above problems – a method of retraceable logic in the socio-political area, if you will.

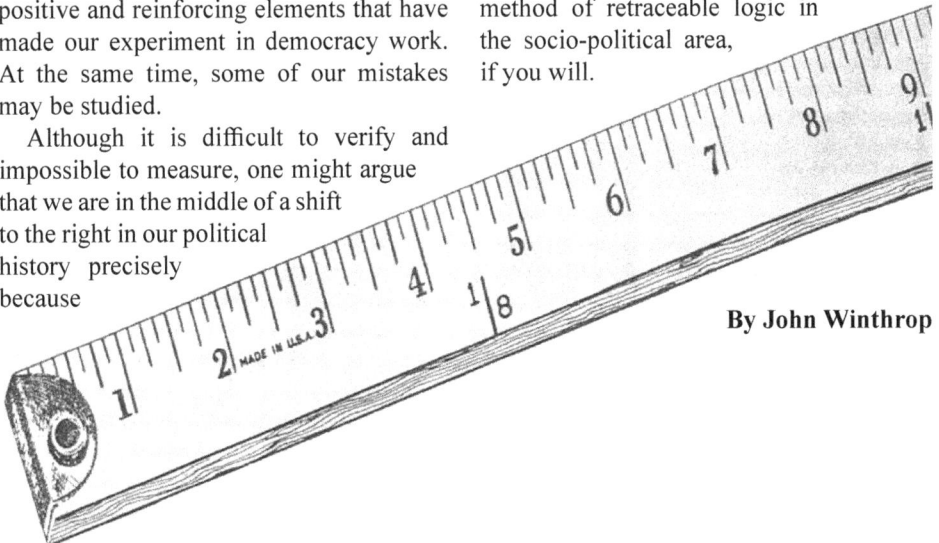

By John Winthrop

Likewise in the investment world, knowledge of history is very important. While the stock market is known to be influenced by hopes, fears and aspirations from one day to the next, a study of history shows us that the long term trend of equity prices is governed primarily by variables which can be measured. Consider the following comparison illustrated in the accompanying box.

The companies selected are simply a random sample of industry-leading corporations, which share certain basic characteristics. During the 1965-1975 span – a period of social and economic turbulence – these companies withstood most of the tests of having superior management. Measurement of growth, profitability and balance sheet strength are all relatively favorable. These companies have prospered despite adversity.

None of the companies listed have been the very best performers on the New York Stock Exchange in any one year. But, they haven't been the worst performers, either. The comparison with the market averages clearly demonstrates, however, that they have been excellent performers as a group.

Asset management is an art form, but it is also a science. As the profession has become more competitive in recent years, it has become clear that the portfolio manager of a pension fund – or any other fund, for that matter – who is governed by a series of analytical disciplines is more likely to be able to boast success over a period of time. No longer is it enough to be captivated by a "story," to outguess the industry group to be favored next, to spot the "turnaround" situation.

The more thoughtful students of equity investments have isolated and listed the variables which they believe influence stock prices. There is no magic list which

Selected issues – ten-year performance

Security	Year-end closing price		Capital gain (loss)	Earnings per share		Earnings gain (loss)	Dividend		Yield gain (loss)
	1965	1975		1965	1975		1965	1975	
IBM	$130	$224	72%	$3.52	$13.35	279%	$1.56	$6.50	316%
Citicorp	14	30	114	0.88	2.81	219	0.50	0.86	72
Merck	36	69	92	0.94	3.03	223	0.60	1.40	133
Warner-Lambert	21	36	71	0.80	2.15E	169	0.45	0.90	100
Sears-Roebuck	66	65	(2)	2.08	3.00E	44	1.50	1.85	23
Exxon*	80	89	11	4.74	11.18	136	3.15	5.00	59
Dow Chemical	26	92	254	1.20	6.75	463	0.60	1.45	142
3M	32	56	75	1.09	2.29	110	0.55	1.35	145
Eastman Kodak	59	106	80	1.53	3.80	148	0.90	2.06	129
Xerox	67	51	(24)	.93	3.07	230	0.18	1.00	456
Mean appreciation over 10-year period (unweighted)			74%			202%			31%
Dow Jones Ind.	969.26	852.41	12%	53.67	74.66	39%	28.61	37.46	31%
S&P 425	98.47	100.88	2%	5.51	8.30E	51%	2.85	3.78	33%

* in 1965, called Standard Oil New Jersey; E: Estimate; Figures as of 2/24/76

provides an easy crutch for the investment advisor. But a common-sense approach, and a look at history, compels the portfolio manager to examine his decision-making process and to discipline his thinking as he structures his portfolio. This process can be logically broken down into four phases:

1. Developing categories of industries. Security analysis and portfolio management begin with an analysis of macroeconomic trends. Once a profile is established, it is a relatively simple matter to develop an idea of which industries will be

Winthrop

favored within the emerging economic environment. If industries are grouped into such categories as consumer staples, credit sensitive, intermediate goods and services, capital goods and consumer durables, appropriate weighting can be assigned to any given group before the stock selection begins.

2. Developing a quantitative screen. Certain measurable characteristics are shared by most of the superior performers on our chart. Most of these variables can be broken down and identified, but the key variables can be lumped in the broad categories of balance sheet strength, growth and, most importantly, profitability. Appropriate weighting can be assigned to columns on a worksheet as a universe of stocks is compared. The process is simplified by developing an end result – a quantitative factor – which can then be used as a negative screen to sort out those companies unworthy of further scrutiny.

3. Developing a qualitative checklist. Every security analyst knows that a wide

variety of considerations is compiled in his own mind to give him an understanding of that most important quality of all – good management. Accounting policies, environmental impact, labor relations, marketing strategies are only a few of the many items which need to be listed in a systematic review of all the considerations involved in evaluating the quality of management. These topics deserve listing exhaustively. The battlefield of investment advisers is littered with the bones of those who neglected a few key considerations before selecting ill-fated securities for clients' portfolios.

We know that the companies listed in the accompanying box have been out of favor from time to time. But, as we look back in history, over the past decade – indeed, over the past century – investors have been richly rewarded by selecting equities of companies having superior management. The exercise of further weeding out those companies which do not adequately pass through the qualitative questionnaire is well worth the time.

4. Technical considerations. Finally, there have been cases where a company has all the desirable characteristics from a fundamental point of view. It is well situated within the economic forecast; it has an enviable record; it has all the ingredients of good management to weather the storms ahead. Yet, a thorough technical analysis gives the warning signal that timing may not be ideal. Again, the effort to array and list technical considerations should be exhaustive and again the effort is well worth it, because timing as well as selection is important in investment decision-making.

It is worth emphasizing that any step-by-step approach equity selection should not be accepted as gospel. It is important, however, to develop some rational, disciplined method in our profession. Whatever method is adopted, it would appear useful to build the approach with a sense of history. This point seems worth stressing in our Bicentennial year, as we ponder the problems of investment management – an occupation which cries out to be governed by good sense, rather than mercurial impulse.

Mutual Funds Forum, February 1977

Know Your Shareholder:
A Challenge for Mutual Fund Management

Sailing a mutual fund through the stormy seas of the 1970s is proving to be a challenging exercise. Many investors have abandoned the ship, while professional money managers agonized, wept or tried to find new jobs.

Operationally, the waters have been anything but calm. There has been no significant relief in the regulatory environment; in fact, the volume of paperwork has intensified. In most cases expenses have mounted, while revenues have declined. And redemptions have increased to troublesome levels.

One thing we have learned from this period is that we must know more about the individual shareholder. Logically, the first step should be to find out the ages, occupations, marital status, incomes and areas of related investment information of the shareholders. Such information should be valuable in aiding management to direct its policies for maximum benefit to the shareholders and to plan its marketing approach.

As President of a medium-sized fund, I felt we must take some action in this area. With the help and support of the directors, the other officers and the operational backup staff at de Vegh Mutual Fund, we developed a questionnaire which was sent to our shareholders. To encourage a good response, the questionnaire was brief, uncomplicated and easy to complete. It was accompanied by a brief letter from me requesting the shareholder's cooperation.

The number of questionnaires completed and returned to us was far beyond our expectations. Over 40 percent of our shareholders took the time to fill out the questionnaire and send it back to us. To us, this was a clear indication that our shareholders seized upon this opportunity to tell management about themselves as a means of communicating with us.

As for the results, the age of our fund's shareholders seemed to be heavily skewed toward the 50-64 group with 44.3 percent of the total respondents. But we were surprised at the low number of young people owning shares, 2.0 percent were under 18 and 13.5 percent were under 34.

As to education, the weighting was very heavy at the post-graduate level, 43.8 percent with 37.0 percent having attended or graduated from college. These two figures verified what we had believed to be true – that the majority of our shareholders were well-educated.

The number of children and the size of households provided additional information for the "consumer profile." Only 12.5 percent of those responding had large families at home, although a great many had some children.

Although the Investment Company Institute reports that 51.1 percent of all mutual fund shareholders are women, this was not the case with us. Only 20.0 percent of our responses were from female shareholders.

The reason most people purchased our fund's shares was to achieve long-term growth at a minimum of expense. This was followed by professional management and diversification.

One statistic that came as a surprise was that 25 percent of our shareholders own shares in other mutual funds. In addition, many shareholders have other types of investments as well. Life insurance, savings accounts, real estate and common stocks were high on the list.

The results also verified the degree of affluence we had expected of our shareholders. Nearly one-third of the respondents had an annual income of over $20,000. In terms of investment goals, retirement, as we had expected, was the dominant motive for investing in our fund. We were surprised that preparing for the cost of children's education was not as conspicuous a reason as we had expected.

Very broadly, the fund's management learned that it had a responsive body of relatively affluent, well-educated shareholders who probably would be receptive to any creative suggestions designed to assist in their financial programs. They appear to be conservative, stable, sophisticated and, most importantly, responsive to communication.

This survey has provided management with some very valuable and useful information, but the real challenge facing us now is how to use this information in creating a marketing strategy. Among the areas currently under study are:

• Broaden our existing investors by offering Keogh plans and individual retirement accounts to a younger group looking ahead to retirement.

• Address women's groups on the subject of mutual funds so that our percentage of female shareholders comes closer to the national figure.

• Initiate a direct mail program to women, to young people and to those who resemble our newly-determined profile.

• Advertise in professional journals.

• Attempt to make the fund better known through a public relations campaign.

Whether of not we use all or a combination of the above, our shareholders have provided us with the navigational tools for us to reach our marketing destination.

Mr. Winthrop is President of de Vegh Mutual Fund, Inc. He is also a member of the Board of Governors of the Investment Company Institute.

Options in Investing

The world of investing is confusing, and all too often women with money to invest haven't any idea of the number of ways their money could be working for them. To demystify the world of finance, the head of a Wall Street firm describes two very different profiles and some of the investment choices open to each.

It is an acknowledged fact that women outlive men. And it's also a fact that women control more than half the wealth in America today. Yet the irony is that many women – often those with significant assets and high incomes – have an inadequate knowledge of money and finances.

If you are earning a salary, paying your bills, saving some extra dollars and controlling all the other mundane aspects of your financial life, you already have a reasonably good idea of how to manage your money. You don't need a primer on balancing your budget – you already have that well in hand.

What you may need is investment advice. You have worked for your money – now your money should work for you. Investing today is both an art and a science, and it is important for you to be aware of the major possibilities. Read the financial page of your local newspaper; investigate investment clubs and seminars offered across the country by leading brokerage firms; and do some in-depth research on any type of venture you're considering.

Adding to the complexity is the fact that inflation constantly reduces our spending power, and any potential investment should be assessed as a hedge against inflation. Even those most wise in the ways of finance can be baffled by the intricacies of real estate, options, various short- and long-term stocks and bonds, art, antiques, gold and jewelry, so a little personal knowledge should be combined with professional advice before you risk your hard-earned nest egg.

The first step in deciding on a plan is to assess your current financial situation. List, along with their values, all of your existing assets: personal effects, a car, your own house, savings accounts, stocks and bonds, mutual funds, etc. Also list your liabilities, including mortgage and car payments, outstanding bank loans and other such fixed expenses. Next, define your financial goals, which could be growth, stability or income.

Each person's financial goals are different, and certain investments are good for certain needs. At a very practical level, a savings bank offers liquidity and safety and is a good place to put funds aside for emergencies. Life insurance, too, is a vitally important investment for women as well as men. Before exploring other, riskier choices, you should be sure that your savings and insurance are adequate for your needs.

To demonstrate a number of investment options which meet different needs, we offer two financial profiles: one if you are a young career-woman, the other if you have a substantial amount to invest.

The Young Careerwoman

Age	25
Dependents	0
Taxable income	$18,000
ASSETS	
Car	$5,000
Personal effects	6,000
Savings	2,000
Group life insurance (paid by employer)	25,000
LIABILITIES	
Car loan	$2,000
Other budgeted expenditures	10,000
Income (after taxes)	12,000
INVESTMENT GOALS	
Growth	Important
Stability	Important
Income	Important

Growth, stability and income are all important to a young career-woman. In fact, you really can't make a choice among them. Your assets must grow to maintain your buying power in an inflationary economy; you can't afford to allow your meager capital to dwindle; and, in terms of long-term well-being and security, you must resist the temptation to increase your current spending.

Let us assume that you amass $5,000, either through a windfall inheritance, as the accumulation of two years' Christmas bonuses, or by cutting expenditures over a period of time and saving. Since $5,000 is a rather small amount to invest in the stock market, and because you are just breaking even budget-wise, investing in individual stocks is probably too risky. Your most obvious choice would be to put the $5,000 in a savings account. However, because of its higher return and its potential for future growth, a mutual fund ia an option you might also consider.

Mutual funds

There are over 800 mutual funds registered for sale, and they vary widely in financial objectives. Since you are looking for growth, you might invest in an income fund which has the dual objective of providing long-term capital growth and current income. The holdings in such a fund generally consist of stocks that have paid good dividends in the past, have a record of increasing dividends and a reasonable expectation of continuing to produce a good return and maintain the value of their shares.

If, on the other hand, you are interested in taking a chance, a growth fund – with its emphasis on companies showing a solid record of earnings improvement – might be the best choice, especially if eventual long-term growth is more important to your financial well-being than current dividends.

In selecting a mutual fund, it is important to make certain that the one you choose is managed by a group which has a variety of funds. The larger groups not only have several funds with different investment objectives, but they also provide you with the flexibility of switching funds at little or no extra cost. Therefore, you could divide your $5,000 between two (or more) funds: one for current income and another to provide long-term growth toward a comfortable eventual retirement, perhaps.

As you earn more money and your assets and net worth grow, this switching factor will enable you to keep pace with your changing financial profile. All the while, you will have professional management of your investment and thus avoid the possible hazard of a drastic market downturn, which could wipe out all of your hard-earned assets if you had initially invested in high-risk stocks on your own.

There are still other choices open if you are willing to take a risk on the $5,000. If you consider it "found money," and if you are secure in your knowledge of the market – or willing to acquire some expertise – your best venture may be the option market. Highly speculative, options consist of "calls" and "puts" and "straddies" and "spreads," all of which mean you are betting on the future rise or fall of the price of common stocks. A "call" is an option to buy a certain stock listed on a major exchange at a prearranged price within a certain time period. A "put" is an option to sell a certain stock at a certain price. "Straddies" and "spreads" are different combinations of the two basic transactions.

One word about the option market: You don't actually own the stock, you merely have an option either to buy or sell it. And the option market is not for the conservative investor – you would have to have an adventurous nature to embark on this kind of speculative venture. High profits are the lure, but the loss of part or all of the $5,000 is a very real risk.

The Established Careerwoman

Age	35
Dependents	1
Taxable income	$50,000
ASSETS	
House	$60,000
Car	5,000
Personal effects	20,000
Savings	5,000
Tax-exempt, no-load municipal-bond mutual fund	30,000
Renewable term life insurance	75,000

LIABILITIES	
Mortgage	$0
Budgeted expenditures	28,000
Income (after taxes)	33,000
INVESTMENT GOALS	
Growth	Very Important
Stability	Important
Income	Unimportant

If this is your financial profile, you already have the makings of a well-balanced estate plan: Your existing assets and investments are sufficient for you to consult with a professional investment advisor and prepare a well-rounded portfolio toward your retirement and to insure a college education for your child.

If you have worked for one major corporation since graduating from college and now move to a better job with another firm, all the money that is vested for you in profit-sharing with the original company becomes yours and should be wisely invested. Or, if your firm has discontinued its profit-sharing program because of recent restrictive government legislation, that money is available to you whether or not you change jobs. Assuming that you have been working for the same corporation for more than 15 years, your profit-sharing could easily approach $100.000 (Another possibility, of course, is that at this period of your life you might inherit a large amount in the form of a house, stocks, furnishings, jewelry, etc.)

With $100,000 to invest, your advisor would probably recommend the following plan: As eventual growth is a very important financial goal, you should invest in consumer growth stocks. These include companies such as cosmetic and toiletry manufacturers, leisure and recreational firms, food industries. Other choices that would be important, especially in today's economy, would be domestic energy and energy-related stocks, regional banks and insurance companies, and office equipment and electronics stocks. All are growing industries, which means growing dividends and rising market values.

Stability and Growth

The rationale for investing in domestic energy stocks is that the U. S. is gradually becoming less dependent on foreign sources for energy supplies. Regional banks and insurance companies are a good risk because they are not issuing loans to Third World nations, a sound, conservative financial policy in view of the political turmoil in most developing countries. Many manufacturers of office equipment and electronics are establishing their headquarters in the "Sun Belt" area of the country, which is booming economically.

For these reasons, an advisor might recommend that your invest in these proportions: 30 per cent in consumer growth stocks, 30 per cent in energy and energy-related stocks, 20 per cent in credit-sensitive stocks (regional banks and insurance companies), 10 per cent in office equipment and electronics stocks.

Thus 90 per cent is devoted to growth, the most important part of your financial goals. Since stability is also important, an advisor might suggest that you invest about five per cent in domestic gold stocks, as there will inevitably be a further devaluation of the dollar. The remaining five per cent could be invested in art or antiques – a hedge against inflation. Bear in mind, however, that the world of fine art is a highly specialized one, so it is wise to develop personal expertise in the area that most appeals to you, and also to rely on the advice of reputable gallery owners and other fine-arts professionals.

Because the amount of art and antiques on the market is finite, values are bound to increase. Regardless of the state of the stock market, there are always wealthy collectors who will pay substantial prices for beautiful art objects, so if anything from snuff boxes to turn-of-the-century lithographs captures your interest, you might start a modest collection. In addition to its esthetic value, good art is a sound investment.

Investment Advisors

Though these two profiles are very different, they do have one thing in common: Both need professional investment help, which becomes more important the more you have to invest. How do you find the right advisor? Simply shop around as you would for a doctor or a lawyer.

Your investment advisor should understand your lifestyle and the things that are important to you.

• ask you banker or lawyer whom he or she recommends. Don't limit yourself to just one or two firms; give yourself four or five choices.
• Carefully read the firms' literature, remembering that such brochures are selling tools
• arrange a personal meeting with an officer of each of the firms.

At these meetings, ask the following questions:
• How old is the firm? Obviously, it should have an excellent reputation and a proven track record.
• How large is the staff and what are their areas of specialization?
• Who are the firm's clients? Do their investment needs and objectives resemble your own?
• What is the background of the person with whom you will be dealing? Education and qualifications are important, and so is compatibility. Your advisor should

understand your lifestyle and the things that are important to you.

• What is the firm's fee or percentage? Fees are usually a percentage of the amount you are investing, and the smaller this is, the higher the percentage.

Then think it over. Never make an on-the-spot decision; no serious advisor would expect you to. Investing money wisely and profitably requires an investment of your time and the willingness to learn – but the rewards are worth the effort.

Editor's note: John Winthrop is the Chief Executive Officer at Wood, Struthers & Winthrop Management Corp., a Wall Street investment advisory firm.

The Money Manager

April 17, 1978, published by The Bond Buyer

Time to Buy Stocks, If It Is Not at Hand, Is Fast Approaching

A long time ago, a shrewd investor found the key to investment success. "Give the public exactly what it wants," he advised. "If common stocks are in demand and everyone is buying them, feed the hungry and sell equities. If, on the other hand, everyone is selling as if the world was about to end, stand up and buy."

Logic supports the approach. If the argument has any merit at all, the stock market today, after a decade of agony, is far closer to being in a buying range than in a selling range.

The investing public is and has been selling stocks with a passion. Distressed by inflation and the debasement of our currency along with the deterioration of our balance of payments, and the stability of the dollar, among other things, investors have created an avalanche of gloom on Wall Street.

Over the past 10 years, stocks have been pummeled down irregularly responding to the after effects of the Vietnam War and the unconvincing leadership in Washington. In recent months, however, the carnage has intensified. On March 10, 1977, the Dow Jones Industrial average totaled 946.73 and on March 10, 1978, it had reached a low of 763.34. The individual investor has been abandoning the stock market with understandable anger, convinced that there is no future in owning equities.

Before others join this long parade, however, it might be worth pausing to see what has been happening to the underlying value of 10 broadly-held companies over the past 10 years. Any observer of the stock market knows that some of these securities have performed poorly in the past, but very few have stepped back and studied the record over a longer time period. First, let's look at the earnings per share record:

	Earnings per share	
	1967	1977
IBM	$4.64	$18.30
Exxon	2.77	5.38
Citicorp	1.06	6.97
ATT	3.79	6.97
General Electric	1.95	4.79
Mobil Corp.	3.81	9.47
Sears	1.26	3.05
Aetna	1.47	7.76
Dow Chemical	.73	3.01
Merck	1.25	3.67

The average (unweighted) progress these companies made over a 10-year period amounts to 202% increase which compares favorably to 95% for the Dow Jones Industrials and 114% for the Standard & Poor's 500.

Recently, investors have paid more attention to the yields of investments in common stocks. Let us look at what has happened to the dividend record of the same companies over the same time period:

| | Dividend | |
	1967	1977
IBM	$1.74	$11.52
Exxon	1.73	3.20
Citicorp	.46	1.06
ATT	2.20	4.60
General Electric	1.30	2.20
Mobil Corp.	1.85	4.20
Sears	.60	1.12
Aetna	.50	1.60
Dow Chemical	.36	1.20
Merck	.80	1.70

Once again, the average of 174% compares rather favorably to the corresponding figures of the 52% and 63% for the Dow and the S&P 500, respectively.

It should be noted that the investor who purchased these stocks 10 years ago and held them would have received a stream of dividends which would have more than kept up with inflation – actually increasing his buying power. In this respect, common stocks of industry leading companies have, in general, offered a measure of protection against inflation.

What has happened to the actual market performance of the 10 listed companies? Their unweighted mean appreciation over the 10-year period has increased 37.6% as against a loss at year-end for the Dow Jones and the S&P 500. The following figures tell the story.

There is no particular magic in the selection of these companies: they happen to be the 10 largest holdings of many major investment management firms such as ours. As a consequence, their past history and future prospects are of keen interest to investment managers.

Capital Gain (Loss)	
IBM	12%
Exxon	41%
Citicorp	64%
ATT	20%
General Electric	4%
Mobil Corp.	47%
Sears	(3%)
Aetna	80%
Dow Chemical	80%
Merck	31%

The figures tell the story. The market performance, while relatively superior, has not come close to keeping up with the earnings gains or dividends payout.

It is undeniably true that the problems seen by investors are very real. We need more convincing proof that our budget will be balanced, that inflation can be brought under better control, and that more definitive leadership will be forthcoming. Global, political and economic problems exist and will not be solved over night.

However, the spotlight should be turned on to what has happened to the stocks of good companies – companies that have demonstrated the ability to grow and even thrive under very adverse circumstances. These are the stocks that many people continue to sell eagerly, but the numbers show that the selling has been overdone.

It can be argued with conviction that it is now time to listen to that faint voice from out of the past telling us to do exactly what the public wants. If this is not the year of market strength, then we are far closer to it than the investing public realizes.

Mr. Winthrop is chief executive officer of Wood, Struthers & Winthrop Management Corp., a subsidiary of Donaldson, Lufkin & Jenrette, Inc.

publication unknown, circa 1970s

A Vacation View of Wall Street and Investment Prospects

Wall Street is generally viewed as the financial capital of the United States, if not of the entire world. Its brokerage houses and banks offer many financial services as well as investment advice and money management. Many would like to believe that this costly advice is perceptive, prudent and will prove very profitable.

As it is the capital of the investment world, it would seem reasonable to assume that Wall Street would offer the most sophisticated and useful advice. Sad to say such is not the case.

Having spent most of my professional life on Wall Street, it is always refreshing to get away to breathe the South Carolina air and think about what has happened to various types of investments over the past decade or two. A log cabin nestling in the pine tress of Allendale County, S. C., seems suitably distant from the noisy canyons of Wall Street to allow some mental stretching to consider not just U. S. bonds and stocks – by far the major focus of Wall Street professionals – but also the other media for investment, like coins, tree-growing raw land, antiques and art.

Recognizing all the hazards of preaching and predicting on these complicated topics let us take a hard look at what has happened:

Coins: Like the stock market itself, coins offer a multitude of possible investments. One can discuss U. S. or foreign coins, numismatic or gold coins, commemorative or ancient coins. For the most part these "collectibles" have done very well in this inflationary age. Gold coins and silver coins have risen (and fallen) in sympathy with precious metals, but the trend has been up in recent years.

One interesting example of a U. S. collectible coin, the pine tree shilling – the first coin in widespread use in America – and one in circulation for nearly 200 years (1652-1852) has gone up in value nearly 10 fold in the last 10 years. Available for a few hundred dollars in 1970, a top grade pine tree shilling will fetch up to $5,000 today.

Art and Antiques: Here, too, there has been an avalanche of buyers bidding up prices. Speculators and collectors have joined the stampede to buy everything from snuff boxes to Queen Anne chairs. In the art market, values have held firm and climbed – particularly at the quality end of the spectrum. Belatedly, Wall Street joined the rush. Banks and brokers acquired art "experts" themselves or developed liaisons with the art world in the hope of steering customers into that unpredictable market. For the most part, however, Wall Street investment advisers simply watched in frustration. The art market flourished while the stock market languished.

David Shepherd, a famous wildlife artist and specialist in the big game of East Africa sold a good sized canvas for $3,000 in 1969 and $30,000 in 1979. The Dow Jones Industrial average went nowhere. Adjusted for inflation, the stock market went down during this period.

Raw Land: Farmers had good reason to ignore Wall Street during this period. Whether they had good years or bad years, the value of their land went up dramatically – better than 10 percent per annum in most locations. Occasionally Wall Street investors studied stock and bond markets but only a few kept tree-growing property in some distant location, such as South Carolina, as an "anchor to windward."

One investor purchased some tree growing property in South Carolina in 1961 for under $100 per acre: in 1970 similar land adjoining it cost him twice as much; by 1980 it cost $1,000 per acre. That pattern is a familiar one to anyone who has studied well-situated real estate of any kind over the same period.

The stock market itself has been a "death march." Men and women graduating from top business schools in the late 1960s and determined to do a good job for their clients, while making a decent living for themselves, have been handed a gigantic and daily study in frustration. As inflation became more and more the most conspicuous fact of economic life, most stocks did not go anywhere. Most of the stock markets around the world, it is important to note, outperformed our own as well. The dollar was weak; productivity lagged; incentives to save or invest in the United States deteriorated.

IBM, the darling of the 1950s and 1960s, and a good example of what was happening to the stocks of good companies, skidded irregularly downward in price related to its earning power. Earnings in fact tripled in the decade of the 70s but the stock fell to a price-earnings multiple of under 10 from over 40 times those per share earnings. Net result: the stock gained no ground.

Today the yield of IBM is greater than that of the average stock and the price, in relation to next year's expected earnings, is at a lower level. All of this applies to one of the greatest companies in the world. The undisputed leader in its industry, with supremely good management and splendid and proven marketing strength, technical excellence and a balance sheet like a battle ship, IBM ranks as a unique company by almost any measurement. Its market price does not reflect this fact!

If the peace and quiet of the South Carolina woods offer any perspective for the embattled Wall Streeter, it is possible to make a general observation.

Inflation is not behind us, although the new administration seems to have turned the economy in the right direction. The serious investor, mindful of the need to hedge, should not discard or sell all his timber property or his collectibles, his stamps or his coins. But most certainly he should not sell the stocks he might still own of leading companies. Investment reserves should be kept marketable, of high quality, and ready until the bond market turns around more definitively than it has to date. When that happens, expect the stock market to move upward with conviction – the U. S. stock market, that is! The pattern of the 70s will not be repeated in the 80s.

Mr. Winthrop is a Wall Street investment manager and a director of several mutual and money market funds.

publication and date unknown

Reaching for quality in the investment business

It is generally accepted in the world of investment management that one shouldn't change style or philosophy when the market begins an obvious rotation in leadership. As those of us in the investment business have seen many times over the past 30 years, it's madness to follow the fashion of the month by hopping from cyclicals to growth stocks; from large companies ("large caps") to small companies ("small caps"); from technology stocks to health-related stocks.

In a word, it's important to develop a sound strategy and then stick to it. The most valid approach is to emphasize quality in the selection of stocks and bonds. But what, exactly, is meant by quality?

For bonds, a good case can be made for selecting those of the highest grade – such as AA or better – as indicated by the rating services. By building a "ladder" of maturities in a bond portfolio, the owner is assured some protection against the changes in interest rates and turbulence of the money markets. A strong defense for a portfolio results.

In the common stock portion of the portfolio the word *quality* or *predictability* of earnings should be used. However, quality in this case goes far beyond its usual, narrow definition.

In recent years certain industry leading, well-managed companies have assumed global importance "strutting their stuff"

around the world, if you will. Some of them are obvious: *Merck*, *Coca-Cola* and *Microsoft*, to name just three.

These companies fall into a very special category of splendid – or high-quality – companies distinguished by strong balance sheets, increasing earnings, a technological edge and, most importantly, excellent management. Although they frequently have other characteristics, these are enough to provide an adequate idea of what is meant when applying the word *quality* to the selection of stocks.

Using the approach of selecting quality stocks and bonds all but guarantees both a strong offense and defense in the construction of a portfolio. Moreover, while used in appropriate portions to suit a client's needs, this approach provides an excellent guide for a fiduciary or a person responsible for the investments of others.

Historic perspective

Ever since the days of the Roman Empire, investors have been preoccupied with the idea of timing markets. The notion of buying low and selling high has had such appeal through the ages that a large group of market students (called "chartists" or technical analysts) devoted much of their energies to timing the market on the purchase and sale of individual stocks.

The founder of one of Canada's oldest investment advisory firms, the late Brian Heward, once said that the key to investment success is to always give the public exactly what it wants. When the public wants desperately to sell, stand ready to accommodate and buy the unwanted issues. Likewise, be equally "helpful" when public sentiment is overwhelmingly on the buy side by selling obligingly.

The trouble, of course, is that the momentum and the psychology of a market is so strong, and at times so overwhelming, that it becomes nearly impossible to be good at market timing – even for the most disciplined of professionals. No one to date has been able to buy at the bottom of the market and sell at the top consistently.

After weighing these considerations year after year, it becomes clear that professional investors can spend their time far more fruitfully by selecting the best companies- – the splendid, well-managed companies, if you will – and then monitoring the progress of those holdings very, very carefully.

Choosing stock is not a matter of buying and holding, but rather of detecting significant changes which will affect the ability of a company to control its destiny. Then stocks must be sold and assets re-deployed.

On the other hand, this approach is not the only valid one. There are those who have been smart or lucky (or both) and conducted a market timing strategy with some success. There are others who have demonstrated over time that the so-called value approach makes sense. These strategists devote their energy to finding those stocks which are undervalued in the market place. Typically, they are selling at prices low in proportion to book value or at a low price in relation to earnings.

Others have invested in bank stocks alone, or in utility stocks alone, or in those of some other industry. If these mutual funds or market segment stocks are held in times of their respective industry's obvious exuberance, the holders will be richly rewarded; at other times they will languish.

There are many investment vehicles of choice, and without exhausting the list of alternatives, there are those who are consumed by the appeal of derivatives or options or currencies or futures or commodities. Some have done very well; most have been made humble.

In conclusion it can be safely said that the investment process is immensely complicated but it can be made understandable. This basic truth is a fact for most professions. Sound investment advice also appeals to one's basic sense of logic.

The future should prove an exciting and challenging time for those of us in the investment business. While the philosophy of sticking with quality – with an appropriate degree of risk aversion through the defense of bonds – may not be the only way to success, it's a mighty good one.

Management Practice Bulletin

October 2002

A Very Full Agenda for Mutual Funds Trustees Belies Current Criticism

John Winthrop, an Independent Trustee of the Pioneer Funds, argues that recent criticism by the financial press of the role of Independent Trustees of Mutual Funds is both unfair and ill informed.

No attempt to list the growing issues confronting independent trustees today can be complete. Over the past year we have seen that even the list of "hot button" items can be elusive. Those of us in the trenches know that our duties are more complex than our counterparts on traditional company boards. A brief view of some of the issues confronting independent trustees of mutual funds might be helpful in giving substance to these general comments:

• Investment Performance – Few, if any, knowledgeable, independent trustees would say they are responsible for performance. After all, the investors purchased the fund because of the manager's reputation, not that of the trustees. However, trustees are responsible to see that the investors have the best possible chance of earning a competitive return. This means they have to constantly monitor the resources and capability of the management company, each portfolio manager and his or her supporting team. In cases of consistently poor performance, the trustees may have to demand changes from the management company – or in extreme cases, even terminate the relationship.

• Disaster Recovery and Money Laundering – With the unthinkable tragedy occurring in September 2001, the trustees have oversight responsibility and must make sure appropriate disaster recovery plans are in place. Similarly, the need for a management company to know its customer base has never been greater – a particularly challenging task for mutual fund managers and trustees alike. Even demographic and economic profile studies are rarely initiated and omnibus accounts are frequently used in the asset gathering process. Nevertheless, the trustees must ensure that a money laundering policy is in place that satisfies the regulatory authorities.

• Code of Ethics and Governance – These subjects have always been of interest to independent trustees, but in a post-Enron environment they must be classified as critical issues. Management companies and trustees stand ready to pounce on any conflict of interest matters in today's world; so is the SEC. Years ago women, African Americans and other minority groups were rarely seen on mutual fund boards. That has changed for the better. Independent trustees must establish their own reasonable compensation level, form their own committees, identify appropriate schedules for meetings, and select qualified individuals to add to their oversight body. Retirement policy has been and is being established by many boards. In like manner, board evaluation procedures are being put in place.

• Audit Committee Charter – Another governance issue is to create a roadmap for the audit committee. This list of assignments includes many duties – a number of which must be ratified by the full board. Deep and up-to-the-minute financial expertise is required. The independence of auditors, legal counsel and even trustees themselves must constantly be monitored.

• Contract Review – This item remains the most important task for all independent trustees. The full burden of protecting shareholders through this annual review process rests with them, and, while they may and should have independent counsel, virtually none is blessed with their own support staff. In large families of funds it is vitally important to allocate expenses properly among funds in a fair manner. The allocation process covers management fees, 12b-1 fees, custody of the fund's investments and shareholder transfer charges as well as less obvious expenses such as ICI dues, insurance expenses, professional fees and Board expense. In addition, the profitability of each fund and the overall complex to the manager must be analyzed and compared.

• Brokerage Allocation, Best Execution and Soft Dollar Review – The commission dollars of each of the funds must be reviewed on a regular basis. This reduction in shareholder return creates and additional "hurdle" above and beyond the expenses discussed above. The trustees must verify that these dollars benefit the shareholders of each fund in the complex. In like manner, getting the best possible price on purchases or sales of fund investments is important. Trustees must be convinced that shareholders are treated fairly and that all trading activity is in compliance with regulations.

• Valuation Issues – Particularly in emerging market funds and those funds investing overseas, many events can cause disruptions in the pricing of stocks or bonds. Procedures for dealing with unpredictable events must be created and consistently acted upon to make certain shareholders, buying or selling, are treated in an equitable manner. The trustees must ensure that each valuation decision be fully documented.

• Style Drift - Potential shareholders should always read the prospectus of any fund they are considering. Of course, this does not always happen. But knowing that each fund has its investment objective and style described clearly in the prospectus, trustees are charged with the responsibility of ensuring that the investment advisors stay on course (today, there are often many different advisors and sub-advisors involved in anyone complex). A technology fund should not begin investing in insurance stocks; a value fund should not slide into a growth stock bias. Trustees are ultimately responsible for guarding against "style drift".

• Credit Analysis – Years ago investment advisors paid too much attention to income statements and not enough attention to the balance sheet. The bear market we have seen in recent years has educated all of us to consider the source of earnings with care. The implication for trustees is to ask questions about the credit review process for all kinds of investments. This can and should be done without micromanaging any portfolio. It is the investment process that must worry the fund trustees.

This list is neither all-inclusive nor the final word on independent trustee responsibility.

The road ahead for independent trustees promises mountains of paperwork, the necessity of good judgment, and an understanding that there are not always easy answers.

publication and date unknown

Changes at U.S. colleges create higher education

College is on the minds of many folks this time of year – particularly those about to leave town and find a new life beyond the familiar boundaries of the past. The college scene has changed just as the world has changed over the past quarter century.

Parents are certainly aware of the changes. In fact it does not seem so long ago that many of us were going off to college ourselves.

But how has the picture changed and what are the distinctive differences between college 25 years ago and college now? No one is an authority on this multifaceted question, but on any list of major significant changes the chances are that the following three would be included :

Computers – Computer technology has swept over campus life just as it has most academic and scientific disciplines. Many colleges require an introductory computer course; most encourage students to develop a familiarity with these machines which now govern our lives.

Diversity – Nearly every campus is more diversified with a greater ethnic and religious and geographic mix of students than it was a quarter of a century ago. An important change has been the higher percentage of students from the Far East, but the overall percentage of students from all over the world has climbed higher.

This change has created the need for adjustment and has caused stress. Cultural and behavioral differences abound. But in general, resilience has been evident and the changes have helped young people to better adapt to the real world.

Competition – The increased competitive environment exists almost everywhere. There have been "battle casualties" but there have also been many cases where students have demanded the best within themselves whether in making a team, participating in an artistic effort, or in getting into a college of their choice.

Despite all of the above – despite all the subtle and not so subtle changes, despite the pressures and the overcrowding, most colleges are better places than they were twenty-five years ago. Institutions of higher learning in the United States today have written a success story of their own. Parents have become aware of this basic fact as they revisit campuses and students have an opportunity to stand on the shoulders of those who have made the journey before and helped build the institutions of higher learning.

John Winthrop, a Greenwich resident, is the founder of John Winthrop & Co., a New York-based trust-management and investment firm. In 1979 he interrupted his career in investment management to work for the Republican Party in the national election campaign.

What are your thoughts on inherited wealth?

Is it a good thing for your descendants and for society? If you feel that there are some dangers involved in large inheritances, what are they and how would you seek to avoid them?

It is certainly true that great quantities of money left to one's children and grandchildren can rob them of their initiative, their energy, and their drive. However, if the proper example is set by the donor-parent or grandparent, inherited wealth can be a good thing for one's progeny, and for society.

Understanding that it is possible to have too much of a good thing, there is no question that an inheritance can provide a certain level of financial self-respect and independence. It can also maximize the contribution one can eventually make to society by providing the funds for graduate school and for a more deliberate choice of a productive career.

In the final analysis, however, providing funds for our children and grandchildren is a leap of faith: It is a way of saying to your successor, "No matter how many temptations there are out there on which you may squander your assets, I think you will be discreet and sensible." It is a way of saying, "I love you and I believe you are made of the right stuff." I am certain that this was the unspoken message from my father when he passed on financial assets to me years ago.

JOHN WINTHROP,
CHARLESTON, SC

MOSTLY ON
THE WORLD

Greenwich Time

date unknown

No business as Usual in China

C"hina Announces Crackdown on Corruption of Local Officials and Cuts or Satelite Communication with the U.S."

This headline floated over the crowds in Times Square in early July. Most people seemed to ignore it, but for anyone who had been to the People's Republic in recent years, the words demanded attention and added to a feeling of immense sadness.

As a member of a delegation of 25 money managers and people with a background in finance from all over the United States, this observer had an opportunity to develop some clear impressions amid a series of banquets, speeches and discussions two years ago. We visited Beijing, Shenyang and Shanghai – in that order – and then returned to the United States by way of Hong Kong.

While the contrast between Hong Kong and the financial and industrial centers of mainland China was striking, all of us were left with a feeling of hope and optimism about China's future. Clearly the situation deserves some re-evaluation today.

Capital formation is very much on the minds of the leaders of China today – even members of the aging leadership. Indeed, one of the reasons we were invited to visit the country was to provide information on how the stock and bond markets worked,

JOHN WINTHROP

Greenwich Time Board of Contributors

how mutual funds and other institutions functioned and how a small business in America developed.

Despite enormous progress in trade and in industrial growth in recent years, the People's Republic of China is only in the earliest stages of attracting capital adequate to her needs. To date the country has paid off debt to the Soviets and established credibility on getting foreign aid and assistance – particularly from Japan. But the real strength of China can only be realized through capital formation accompanied by modern capital markets which will sustain its economic growth.

Two years ago, the People's Republic had begun to look outward to be receptive to new ideas and to apply them – even if these ideas came from a capitalist's notebook. A meeting with Zhang Jing Fu, top finance minister in Beijing, is worth remembering.

Here are some quotes from my journal:

1. The open door policy will continue.

2. The government appreciated our visit.

3. There is need to exchange views on all areas of endeavor – not just business.

4. The job of feeding one billion people has been enormous, but the plans for the future are enormous.

5. From 1980 to 1990 the GNP will double.

6. Attracting capital is important to China.

7. There is recognition that incentives are needed: profits will be shared.

8. America's experience will be valuable to China.

What has changed? Clearly the events in Tiananmen Square and the pica for democracy, along with all the poignancy and symbolism of the Statue of Liberty constructed by the demonstrators have created a watershed. Credibility has been damaged; capital formation within China has suffered a real set back – of a magnitude of several years; knowledge will now be shared more slowly; the grid of financial institutions – banks, brokerage firms, insurance companies – will develop more gradually.

Yet it is difficult to conclude that all is lost. On the contrary, we left with a conviction that the basic character of the Chinese people which has very little to do with politics, provided promise for the longer term future. The teamwork, the self-discipline, the basic business instincts of the shopkeepers, so visible in the market places of Shanghai and elsewhere, suggested that the Chinese people were and are, in their bones, good businessmen.

Beyond this, members of the younger generation have seen better housing, more scooter bikes and cars and, most importantly, more television. They have learned something about the tradition of free choice and liberty in other parts or the world – or certainly the elite and educated younger people of the cities have learned much. With television and improved communication, these lessons and these ideas will eventually reach the rural sections of the country; also, the truth of what has happened in some of the urban centers will reach the countryside.

In hindsight, we should have paid more attention to the young people who desperately wanted to communicate. They would engage us in conversation at every opportunity, asking about our educational institutions, our work, and our life in the United States.

These were the signals that our group failed to interpret and understand fully. There was an enormous level of frustration and discontent among many of the people we met, but none of us could ever anticipate what has happened in recent weeks in the People's Republic. Indeed, several of the top China scholars in the country miscalculated what was to happen.

Now that the tragedy has developed beyond the expectations of many observers, one must still conclude that the long term future of China holds promise, The growing pains will be very real; the aging leadership of today will remain out of touch with the people; progress has suffered a big setback, But in the final analysis it is the energy and the ingenuity of the younger generation that provide solid hope for the future. The government will change and credibility will be restored. We have not heard the end of the story by any means, and many of us will be looking for more encouraging news out of China in the years ahead.

John Winthrop, who maintains homes in Greenwich and South Carolina, is the founder of John Winthrop & Co., a Charleston, S.C.-based trust-management and investment firm.

Greenwich Time

date unknown

How the Chinese Perceive Americans

A three week trip to China is hardly enough to provide the American visitor with an in-depth knowledge of Chinese attitudes toward the U.S. Indeed, if one speaks with three people on such an evasive subject, one is likely to get four opinions. Nevertheless, six days of discussions on various aspects of investment and finance, along with several banquets and many chances for individual meetings, gives even the most casual observer an idea of how we are perceived.

The characteristics of Americans break down into several categories. We are seen appropriately as having strengths and weaknesses and, while the following list is not all inclusive, it gives some idea of the bottom line of several conversations.

Among the perceived weaknesses are the following:

• Impatient – Americans are results-oriented. "Do we or do we not have a deal" seems to be the mindset too frequently. At best we think in terms of decades. With a history dating back thousands of years, a ten-year period or a twenty-five year period is simply viewed differently in China.

• Ill-prepared – Americans come to China in groups and delegations to discuss a variety of subjects. Frequently, in the

JOHN WINTHROP

Board of Contributors

world of business and finance at least, we are ill-prepared for our meetings. (Our delegation was no exception.) At a very fundamental level this fault is the result of a total lack of grounding and education in Chinese culture and history. Very few Americans speak Chinese; many Chinese speak English.

• Inflexible – When engaged in actual negotiations, Americans appear inflexible all too frequently. The legalistic and contractual demands appear unreasonable. A willingness to start a business relationship in a small city and then build on it in an atmosphere of mutual trust, as the Chinese prefer, does not exist on our side all too often.

• Superficial – The term "fair weather friends" cannot be easily translated in the People's Republic, but Americans are labeled this way in the minds of the Chinese. Our delegations come and go, friendships are made, and all is forgotten far too often. Worse yet, promises are not kept. If the Chinese are suspicious of Westerners, it is because there is a long history of unkept promises. Americans must be mindful of this fact as they take the long trip across the Pacific.

But we must not leap to the conclusion that we are neither liked nor respected in the People's Republic. This is not true. Among all foreigners, Americans are probably liked and respected best. America has clear strengths. Among them:

• Approachable – It is heard around the world and it is most certainly heard in China: Americans are friendly, open, and approachable. While all outsiders are viewed as barbarians by the Chinese, we are the least barbaric. The fact that we are approachable is clearly appreciated and opens the door to communication.

• Management – Our knowledge and skill in management is admired in the People's Republic. Upon several occasions, we were told that our knowledge of financial markets and of managing investments was of great interest. In addition, our approach to the management of a business is admired despite differences in philosophy and despite different political systems.

• Powerful – closely related to our management skills, our power, our wealth, our industrial and military might is respected. The Chinese people are very proud and feel that over time, they will be ahead of us. Meanwhile this characteristic counts as a clear plus in the balance sheet of strengths and weaknesses.

• Positive – Our upbeat, optimistic and positive attitude has helped bolster a good relationship over time between our countries. Our positive approach to life, once again, is viewed as a national trait. It is appreciated and admired.

The emerging picture is mixed. Most delegations returning from China do so with mixed results. Most members of our delegation returned with some questions as to the lasting value of the discussions we had. We felt that a beginning was established in a dialogue. (We even formed an investment club for eventual investments in Chinese bonds and stocks as an indication of our faith in the recent initiatives and in the Open Door policy.) Some members of our group will return to mainland China; others will not. Those who do return and who develop friendships on a people-to-people basis are likely to find that those friendships will be very solid. Loyalty is an enduring trait of the Chinese people.

John Winthrop, a Greenwich resident, is the founder of John Winthrop & Co., a New York-based trust-management and investment firm. He recently visited China as a member of a people-to-people delegation of finance.

Greenwich Time

date unknown

In the view from Europe,
U.S. has room to improve

Any effort to portray America as seen by today's Europeans is bound to be imperfect. There are slight differences in perception from country to country and from person to person.

Nevertheless, after talking with a number of shrewd observers on a whirlwind visit to the continent, it is possible to develop a list of pluses and minuses, of assets and liabilities that paints a reasonably interesting picture of America. In the plus column, most Europeans would agree that the United States possesses several strengths. Among them:

Strength – The reaction to the Iraqi invasion of Kuwait has underscored the awareness of our raw military power. At whatever economic cost, America's reaction is viewed as a awesome and our strength is viewed as the backbone of the alliance.

Stability – In an uncertain world, our democratic form of government has withstood all kinds of pressures and changes and has emerged after Watergate and Vietnam with renewed respect among most Europeans.

Capitalism – While we have moved into a more global economy in recent years, the grid of financial institutions and the liquidity of the various markets in America constitute a beacon for capitalism. The recent triumph over Communism has

JOHN WINTHROP

Greenwich Time Board of Contributors

emphasized the notion that America's brand of capitalism is a strength.

Marketing – The extraordinary degree of acceptance of such items as Coca-Cola, blue jeans, and Disney – globally and in Europe – bears witness to our skill as marketers. More than just products, we seem to have exported our culture worldwide for good or for bad. In any event, marketing skills must be considered one of our strengths.

People – If viewed as a bit naive, Americans are still greeted warmly in Europe. We are, in general, considered friendly and we are well liked – perhaps more so than in past decades when our prosperity was more conspicuous.

Despite these and other assets, however, Americans have qualities which clearly

77

would be considered negatives. These would include:

The Budget – Our inability to solve our budget deficit problem is more than just a petty annoyance to most Europeans. In undercuts our economic strength and threatens our future prosperity. Our budget problem is a clear blemish.

> **Our inability to solve our budget deficit problem is more than just a petty annoyance to most Europeans. It undercuts our economic strength and threatens our future prosperity.**

Laziness – Our friends worry that our work ethic, which contributed to our development in the past, may be wanting. The question is put in high relief when we are compared to our low-wage earners of the energetic countries of the Pacific Rim. Our education system does not seem to be steering us in the right direction.

Drugs – While not exclusively an American problem, the drug culture and accompanying side effects have caught the attention of the Europeans. The civil unrest in our major cities, the increased violence, are seen as major negatives. Our friends pray for further success of the president's war on drugs.

Insularity – Our geographic location limits our vision in the world community. We are not fluent in other languages; our diplomatic skills and our global awareness need improvement sometimes.

Procrastination – Our inability to face up to problems, be it gas conservation or most importantly, environmental protection, seems to be an American trait. Indeed, the decay of our cities' infrastructure of roads, bridges, and subways seems to provide further evidence of our instinct to put off problems.

The events of the past weeks seem to have regained some respect among our friends overseas. In a sense, our leadership role in the western world has been reasserted. Looking to the future, however, a unified Europe will be defining the challenges of leadership once again. The description of American assets and liabilities will remain a moving target in the years ahead.

John Winthrop is the founder of John Winthrop & Co., a Charleston, S.C.-based trust-management and investment firm.

publication and date unknown

Britons Express Views on U. S.

Three-hundred-fifty years after the founding of Boston, America and Great Britain have seen great changes come upon themselves and one another. Each has experienced periods of military dominance and humiliation; economic vitality and weakness, assertiveness and questioning. But 1980, the year of Boston's birthday party, provided an appropriate time to tour Great Britain and ask a wide range of British friends about how they viewed America.

The responses were fascinating – sometimes offered with conviction, sometimes haltingly, but with a remarkable degree of consistency and always with compassion. The responses broke down as follows:

Strong Points of America:

• **Military Strength** – While not always viewed as the solution to all problems, our military strength is seen as awesome and obvious. Arms control was a frequent topic of conversation.

• **Natural Resources** – Particularly when compared with the raw materials of England, America's wealth of natural resources provides great security in an uncertain world. Some felt we took this blessing for granted far too often.

• **Economic Strength** – Capitalism has worked for us. As the Prime Minister tries to nudge Great Britain away from socialism, with considerable pain, this basic fact of life seems recognized – despite our recession, despite our unemployment, and despite inflation.

• **Generosity** – Despite any of our faults, our generosity and our friendliness seems broadly recognized and appreciated. The Marshall Plan is only the most obvious example; this trait is viewed as part of our national character.

All is not viewed favorably in America by our British friends in today's world, however. After some prodding, people we met volunteered some thoughts on our weaknesses. Among them…

• **Arrogance** – Our various strengths seem to give us a heavy handedness from time to time which is not appreciated. This quality can be seen occasionally in our foreign policy and even among our tourists.

• **Violence** – Too frequently we appear to reach for the easy solution in a complicated world. Our streets and cities are viewed as somewhat unsafe; we have had more than our share of public figures assassinated;

we tend to lean toward military rather than toward diplomatic solutions in our relations with adversaries.

• LACK OF LEADERSHIP – We are not producing the quality of leaders we need if we are to assume leadership in the western world. Not enough of our better educated people are going into public service.

On many of these points the strengths and the weaknesses were combined. The emphasis varied but the extent to which the characteristics of the American people were viewed similarly was striking.

Clearly the development of such a scorecard in 1980 was a more complicated task than listing the pluses and minuses of the New World in 1630 when no one in England had much of an idea about how the Indians behaved and most considered the unknowns of the wilderness much less appealing than the comforts of home.

December 26, 1983

President, Imagine What the Russians Think

To: President Reagan
From: A concerned citizen

We are living in a world of high risk. As a loyal Republican, an involved environmentalist and a father of three boys, I am making a serious effort to focus on the future of life in America and on this planet.

At the beginning of your Administration, inflation threatened the stability of our society with far greater intensity than it does today. That basic fact of life made many of us work for you and for the Republican Party. You acted swiftly and courageously to bring this menace under far better control. Today, the threat of nuclear war transcends all other problems.

Sadly, very few Americans have been to the Soviet Union or have had the opportunity to communicate with Russians on a person-to-person basis. Among those of us who have been fortunate enough to travel to the Soviet Union, the vast majority have returned with the conviction that Russians and Americans need to get to know each other to communicate more rather than less, to compare the differences between our systems of government and perhaps even to make the important effort to see how the world looks from the other's point of view.

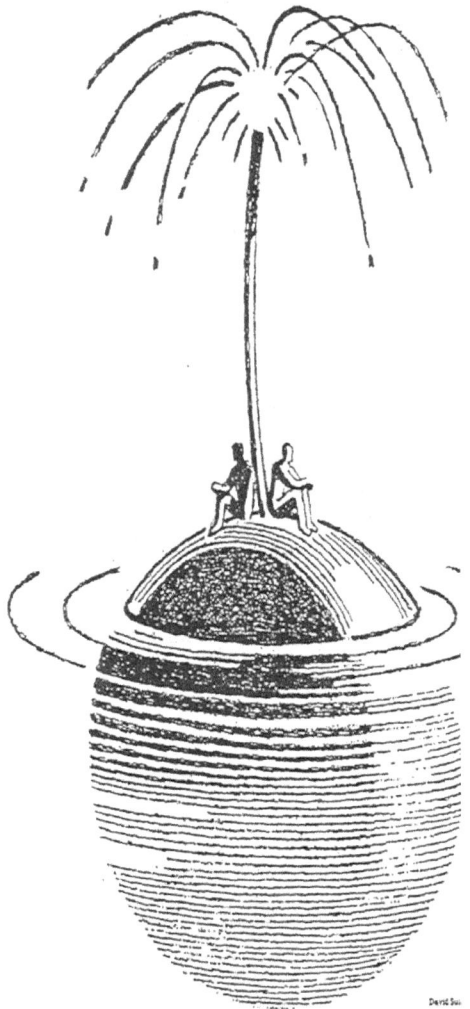

81

As you know so well, truth and disclosure weigh heavily on the side of freedom and democracy. Less clear is what we should be doing in response to the threats caused by the Soviet Government.

Twenty years ago, the placement of missiles in Cuba created a situation in which we felt that weapons of mass destruction were too close to our shores. The lead time for a retaliatory response would have been too short for us to tolerate. Today, most of us agree that President John F. Kennedy acted creatively and responsibility to remove that threat. Given that experience, one would think that we could make a better effort to understand that what must be going through the minds of the people of the Soviet Union as we move our missiles closer to their border.

We don't need to travel to the Soviet Union to relate to the people of that country on this basic level. The idea that we are increasing our security by this response to the Soviet buildup is difficult to grasp for some of us. Everything depends on the willingness of the Soviet Union to return to the negotiating table. Meanwhile, we are shortening the fuse while, at the same time, increasing the possibility of miscalculation.

There seems to be remarkably little effort to put ourselves in the shoes of the people of the Soviet Union, to ponder the fact that they feel surrounded and live with a siege mentality, to re-examine our own assumptions. In my opinion, there has been too little indication of flexibility and too much reliance on tough talk.

As you are aware, great changes in our society have come about through the voluntary initiatives of the citizenry. Advances in the area of civil rights and even in bringing the Vietnam conflict to a close began when growing numbers of Americans developed strong ideas on subjects of great controversy. You have applauded and encouraged initiative from the grassroots. It is my hope that you will listen carefully to those of us who have supported you in the past and want to continue to support you now.

At the present time, we are faced with a problem of balancing the risks of de-escalation against those of increasing world tension. Forgetting for a moment the fact that less money on defense would contribute toward balancing the budget and allowing bolder initiatives in addressing human needs, there might be a measured and beneficial response if we began to change our course.

Obviously, there are risks in making concessions, Mr. President, but today Russians and Americans live in the bull's-eye of missiles.

I submit that this reality is destroying the quality of life in both societies.

A bold effort to reach out and develop greater cooperation in space travel, more trade, increased travel exchange on a people-to-people basis would be both timely and appropriate.

Some of us who support you will be vocal because we care very much about the kind of world we leave after our generation has departed the scene.

The risks and the tradeoffs demand our attention and require clarity of thought on the part of our leaders.

I urge you and your advisers to re-examine your assumptions, and pray that you will have the courage to consider modifying your course.

John Winthrop is president of John Winthrop and Company, a New York investment firm, and is a registered Republican.

Greenwich Time

Thursday, February 23, 1984

Restless Republican separates good and bad

With some hesitation, I am beginning to engage myself in the debate to save the world from nuclear devastation:

...because I feel that great changes in our society come from individual citizens working together;

... because I worry that the macho self-righteous side of the American character is gaining the edge over our generous and perceptive quality;

...because it makes common sense as well as ethical sense to put ourselves in the shoes of our adversaries and to try to see the world as they see it;

... because I believe the Russians don't want war any more than we do.

As a member of the so-called establishment, I am a Republican and a businessman. Freedom of thought and expression, free trade and free enterprise, profits and prosperity – all are good in my view. Repression, dictatorship and authoritarianism are bad. In addition, I believe that spending beyond one's means, burdening our children and grandchildren with debt and creating arms that can destroy the world many times over are bad.

As a father of three boys, I am increasingly concerned about the quality of life for my children. When they were younger, they equated toughness with respectability. Now they are learning that showing kindness and attempting to understand others generally improves the quality of their own lives.

Our nation is still very young it seems – just as my boys were a few years ago. Self-reliance is part of our national character. It has been said that we are still a frontier society, and perhaps we are. However, we have reached a point where we must rapidly gain a better understanding of the weapons in our arsenal. We must learn that tough talk provides limited benefits. I submit that as a nation as well as individuals, we must make more of an effort to put ourselves in the shoes of our potential enemies.

Several years ago I went to the Soviet Union with a friend. The people we met were industrious, curious and friendly. Having seen the horrors of war, the older people were vocally and passionately against conflict.

We returned from the Soviet Union more convinced than ever that our system of government was superior to theirs. The exchange of views was enormously important on both sides. It remains clear to me and to most Americans who have visited Russia that our system works; theirs doesn't.

Today we are governed by an administration that has restored vitality to our economy and tames, at least temporarily, the menace of inflation which threatened to shred the fabric of our society. These are major accomplishments and deserve the praise and respect of all Americans, in my view.

At the same time, huge sums have been poured into our military establishment. Our national debt has reached a frightening level. The arms race has become more costly and hazardous. The reaction time to nuclear attack has been abbreviated while the chances of miscalculations have multiplied. Our long-term economic health has been threatened by the record deficit. It is difficult for me to comprehend how more nuclear weapons adds in any way to our national security.

While not an antiwar activist, I am convinced that more – many more – exchanges at all levels between Soviets and Americans will improve the chances of peace. Conversely, mutual distrust and perpetuation of the arms race destroys the quality of life.

Obviously the conclusion is that all of us who feel strongly on these matters must speak out. The voice of moderation in America must be heard and we must involve ourselves in the most important debate of our times. We must not fear the "better dead than red" tough guys who choose to make us feel cowardly; neither must we cringe from challenging the huge appetite of the military. We have too many bombs, too much military spending, and not enough emphasis on trying to understand the temperament and viewpoint of the Soviet people during this critical time in our history.

John Winthrop, a Greenwich resident, is president of John Winthrop and Co., a New York investment firm.

date unknown

'Heavy' problems and answers the candidates should have given

An attentive observer of the presidential campaign learned relatively little about the fundamental problems facing our country and, indeed, the world. We learned a little about honesty in filing tax returns about the need to "stand tall." More substantively we learned something about two difficult approaches to our budget and about two different approaches to the other nations of the world.

But how about the really heavy questions. Among them:

1. How is America going to address herself to the growing danger of nuclear war?

2. How is the United States, champion consumer and champion polluter, going to show the way to developing a global approach to the environmental problems, which also threaten life's existence on this planet?

3. How is the growing population problem of the world going to be solved more effectively through international cooperation?

4. How is the global debt as well as the national debt problem going to be solved in a way that will not cripple the poorer nations of the world and generations of the future?

That's a pretty good sample of the "heavies." Admittedly, none of the above is an easy problem to solve. It is even possible that orthodox approaches to the above dilemmas will not work. Even if we had been blessed by more discussion of these subjects, it is likely that the paths to solutions would have been politically unpalatable to both candidates.

It would be refreshing to hear some shorthand solutions to these scary problems – the ones which truly affect the future of mankind. For openers, with the full understanding that each solution needed detail and development, consider the following:

1. The threat of nuclear war is the number one issue of our time. We must recognize that unilateral disarmament with destruction of all nuclear weapons is the only way out of our nightmare. Our form of government – the democratic society – is the only one with the strength to embark on this course. Therefore, we must engage ourselves in the current discussions with the Soviets with confidence and with a high sense of urgency.

2. We have consumed and polluted long enough. Henceforth, the United States will develop a clear and precise plan for

water and air improvement. Forests and farmland, fisheries and rivers and lakes will be restored within the grand design for restoring the environment. Pollutants and hazardous waste will be destroyed. We will work with other countries and the appropriate international bodies in developing a heightened sense of urgency. Consumption and travel may need to be restricted. Ownership and use of cars in cities, for example, may be restricted along with certain extravagances in favor of the higher purpose of saving ourselves from choking on fumes and facing the ruination of acid rain. Military savings will be used to finance this effort.

3. In like manner, the growing population of the world must be recognized for what it is – the root of many other problems – and plans must be put into place to feed existing people, to educate those beyond our borders about the need to control their population growth, and finally to finance birth control for those who cannot afford it. The U.S. will spearhead this effort in the Third World. Despite all the obvious problems with this approach, the risks of our current course are heavier. Once again savings from the military budget, which will de-escalate rapidly, will help finance this demographic action plan, to be given a far higher priority on our national agenda.

4. Financially, as well, the time bomb will be defused. The global debt problem will be monitored and studied more carefully than in the past so that more people will develop a better understanding of this problem, which threatens to pit poor nations against stronger ones. Banks cannot be asked to capitulate, but they can be urged forcefully to exercise better management in terms of guidelines for overseas loans. Clearly, the current problem will take a long time to cure with less stringent payback plans than

originally perceived. As for the national debt, we will face this problem head-on. We will force a balanced budget within the next decade and allow ourselves the opportunity to give future generations renewed hope. A thousand doubts and criticisms could be launched against the articulation of the real problems and over the proposed solutions. But the candidate running on such a platform would get this observer's vote next time around.

Johh Winthrop, a Greenwich resident, is the founder of John Winthrop & Co., a New York-based trust-management and investment firm. In 1979 he interrupted his career in investment management to work for the Republican Party in the national election campaign.

date unknown

Courage in the face of terrorism

Tonight, while watching television, I learned that a bomb had been planted in Boston Garden before the Boston Bruin hockey game against a team from the Soviet Union. The bomb was detonated; no one was injured; the Soviets won the game. This was all we were told like so many other news items, the information was inadequate but, upon reflection, it seemed worthwhile jotting down some thoughts directed toward those who saved the day.

Mercifully, you found the bomb and detonated it. Those risking their lives by serving on bomb squads never get the credit they deserve in an age of increasing terrorism. The news item neglected to mention this. Somehow your courage offset the cowardice of those who planted the bomb. You and your partners should be recognized and congratulated.

In recent years it has become increasingly obvious that life is so very fragile.

With terrorism on the rise we must admit to ourselves that in a free society we will never be able to buy total security. We are all vulnerable.

At the root of terrorism lies suspicion, distrust, desperation, many poorly understood emotions and fanaticism about a cause. Somehow sports and sports events should diffuse rather than perpetuate the darker side of the human spirit.

JOHN WINTHROP

Board of Contributors

Sports are uniquely important in the United States and the Soviet Union. They create an obvious opportunity to bridge misunderstanding between the people of both countries. This process requires nurturing and building. Although the governments of the Soviet Union and the United States are obviously dissimilar, anyone who has actually visited Russia can spot the similarities among our peoples. Many opportunities for friendship exists, although the desire to excel and to compete is strong in both countries. If there was any communication among the players in Boston Garden after the game, the news item had no room for this type of comment.

Most importantly, we are faced with a real opportunity after the Reagan-Gorbachev meeting to seek a better understanding with the Soviets. Cultural, scientific cooperation, and sports events can foster this understanding upon which the future of the human race may well depend.

We have a chance to see better understanding among people rather than hatred come out of a hockey game. You and others like you who have saved us from tragedy in Boston should be thanked for giving us yet another chance to think through these fundamental truths.

John Winthrop, a Greenwich resident, is the founder of John Winthrop & Co., a New York-based trust-management and investment firm. In 1979 he interrupted his career in investment management to work for the Republican Party in the national election campaign.

publication and date unknown

Mexico observed: immense problems and concrete progress

Returning to Greenwich from a brief trip to Mexico in November 1984 – after being away for a long time – generates a feeling of hope and concern about our neighbor to the south. The maternity wards are operating at full capacity in Mexico. Economic problems are immense. Environmental and pollution problems are fierce.

Chapultapec Park in Mexico City is a popular picnic area for Sunday strollers. Today, cars squeeze into the overcrowded parking lots and empty as many as ten to twelve riders. When they spread out on the grass or cluster around a restaurant table, the proportion of babies and children always seems high – a harbinger of the demographers' predictions of more than thirty million in population by the year 2000. Outside the city, squatters blanket the hillsides, living in subhuman conditions with inadequate food and no facilities.

Inside the city, traffic swarms in all directions generating enough soot and fumes to pollute the environment and create growing respiration problems among the inhabitants – the same as New York, Los Angeles and other cities, only worse.

Whether one travels within Mexico City or outside, the basic economic problems, so familiar in the developing nations of the world, are omnipresent – unemployment and low income, peddling and begging, inadequate housing. The drumbeat of problems is louder in the poor rural countryside and in the outskirts of Mexico City. But the problems are there, and the population is growing by the day everywhere.

Yet President Miguel de la Madrid is sounding an upbeat theme, broadcasting that his country is moving toward recovery. Significant savings, he says, will reduce total indebtedness by 280 billion pesos ($1.4 billion). At the same time, he points out, the surplus in the trade account has risen to an equivalent of nearly $14 billion, with foreign exchange income from tourism running 39 percent greater than that of 1983.

Low income groups are benefiting from a national housing development program. Food production, as well, is greater than last year, and the country today is self-sufficient in wheat, beans, sugar, coffee, vegetables and fruit. Most significantly, the huge foreign debt, relating to excesses of the past, has been restructured. Realism about meeting obligations has been stressed by the president.

Despite all of the proclaimed achievements, de la Madrid cautions against overconfidence. He knows there is much to be done in the remainder of his six-year term. Indeed, the impartial observer must take a sober view.

The hard realities are difficult to escape. The purchasing power of the working class has not improved. Corruption in government must be purged from the system. It may have worked its way "into the bones" some believe – into the very structure of government.

Environmental problems must be faced more directly. Air quality as well as water quality - and quantity – demand attention. In nearly all societies environmental problems never seem to receive much attention until they reach crisis stage. Today cab drivers in Mexico City are beginning to talk about the effect of the fumes of the traffic on the lives of their children.

The birth rate problem is, of course, the most fundamental problem of all. The religious, historic and cultural heritage appears nearly impossible to bend, just as it does in so many other nations of South America and Africa.

Children are everywhere to be found in Mexico, and their numbers are conspicuously high in relation to adults. They are warm and friendly and better behaved in many cases than children in other countries. The Mexicans as a people, in fact, are friendly and kind for the most part. In the years ahead, they will also need to be patient and resourceful.

Departing Mexico City. airplanes fly over the gray masses of squatters' huts enshrouded in smog. The visitor cannot help but be focused on the future in viewing this sad spectacle. The consequences of the outcome are vitally important for Mexico and for us. Despite its cultural, economic and political differences, Mexico is in partnership with us – more so, in fact, than ever before.

John Winthrop, a Greenwich resident, is the founder of John Winthrop & Co. a New York-based trust-management and investment firm. In 1979 he interrupted his career in investment management to work for the Republican Party in the national election campaign.

Saturday, July 24, 198?

Argentine love mixed with English roots

The recent tide of violence in the South Atlantic created a high level of anguish for the United States. Long before President Kennedy's ringing eloquence on the Alliance for Progress, we were trying to establish bridges of understanding and cooperation with the various countries of South America. At the beginning of the Reagan Presidency, overtures were made to Mexico and to our Latin American friends to create stronger ties.

And yet our heritage, our culture, our society is linked irrevocably to Great Britain. Our young country was developed largely by people of British stock; our language, our legal system, our institutions have the imprint of England; we have stood by one another through times of hardship and conflict over the past 100 years.

With all of the above as a background, I left Greenwich to visit Argentina on a working holiday some time ago and found it to be a land of fascinating contrasts – rich people and poor people; mountains and flatlands; gigantic urban sprawl around Buenos Aires and unspoiled wilderness around the Valdez Peninsula and elsewhere. The country is rich in natural resources, nearly self-sufficient – and yet the people are desperately disorganized in their efforts to exploit those resources. The people from Argentina struck me as being proud but with appealing humility and charm at times. Along with all of this, the people of Argentina clearly have the passion of most of their Latin American neighbors. I was enchanted by the country and by the people.

More recently I made a new friend from Argentina – a young girl from a large family of modest means living on the outskirts of Buenos Aires. We met through the Christian Children's Fund. Now I correspond with her on a regular basis.

Despite my love of Argentina my roots are in England. My family came from a small hamlet north of London. On a fairly regular basis I make a pilgrimage to that out-of-the-way community. The people are rural, uncomplicated, friendly and, above all, loyal to Americans who take the time to visit. Life moves at a slower pace in the British countryside; the roots run deeper; families have been plowing the same fields for centuries. The visiting American finds the trip a welcome relief from the Lexington Avenue subway and comes back enriched by the experience.

Letters from a friend in Groton, Mary Gates by name, conveyed a sense of horror over the war. She recognized that international law must be respected and yet she was keenly aware of the political picture within Great Britain. Mary is an intelligent woman and a dear friend. We have corresponded over the past decade.

The letters from Argentina have been slower in arriving recently. My little friend, Sandra, sent me a note in her childish scrawl with some pictures drawn at the bottom of the page. The images were of flowers, a garden, and a girl with orange hair – carefully drawn and quite recognizable. The scenes were peaceful.

The yearning for peace is obvious to anyone who was in communication with either side in the conflict. It is only by accident that I was in simultaneous contact with both sides when the war over the Falkland Islands dominated the headlines. On a human level our national dilemma was made even more poignant while corresponding with friends. The conflict has not been mentioned in my letters to Sandra, nor in hers to me. As a third grader she is far more interested in trying to improve her grades than in trying to develop an understanding of why her country was at war.

Mary Gates, on the other hand, had much the same kind of reaction to the fighting as most enlightened adults. She recognized how the tempo of the conflict moved up, fueled by national pride. At the same time she recognized the violence is simply not an appropriate solution to a problem. Looking at Sandra's pictures and reading her last letter so full of hope for the future, on can only conclude that war is an unacceptable solution to problems, particularly in a nuclear age.

John Winthrop, a Greenwich resident, owns an investment firm in New York City.

Greenwich Time

date unknown

Letter to the Editor:
The Iraq Situation

To the editor:

A conversation with a diplomat from Holland added insight to this difficult situation. My friend, the ambassador, feels it is essential that the United States continue to work in concert with the United Nations.

President Bush's swift response to the Iraqi invasion of Kuwait was masterful, he felt. But we must push the diplomatic initiatives through the United Nations to the outer limits before taking the military option. This means giving the United Nations a chance to be fully effective.

President Bush's instinct to work with other leaders seemed instinctive and brilliant in the early hours after the invasion. President Reagan would have been far more inclined to work alone, it was felt.

While the outcome is by no means certain, and while many challenges lie ahead before the United States can approach any of its stated objectives in the conflict, it is safe to say that we are witnessing a watershed event. After the events of these weeks, there are likely to be new alliances and new patterns of cooperation – our relationship with the Soviets, the Saudis, and the United Nations itself, to name only a few. It may also help force a redefinition of the role of NATO.

While it is difficult to perceive much in the way of a silver lining from the chaos launched by Saddam Hussein, it is becoming clear that there will be a new sense of urgency surrounding such matters as energy conservation, the balancing of the budget, and even achieving world order.

As Europeans try to prepare themselves for the difficult days ahead there appears to be considerable good will toward America. In my discussion with my diplomat friend and others it appeared that there might be some quiet concern as well. President Bush has defined the job ahead of us as well, but our friends want us to exhibit the tenacity, good sense, and courage to sustain the Mid-East initiative, to face up to our financial problems and solve them and to develop a convincing energy policy and stick by it. All of this will require character.

John Winthrop
GREENWICH

MOSTLY ON
TRAVEL

—— The Boston Globe ——

Sunday, September 1, 1963

Far East Diary I
Saigon Observer Says U.S. Should Pull Out

Saigon in Viet Nam is the center of a crisis that has serious implications for the United States and the free world. In the following article, the first of a series, John Winthrop, a young Bostonian, gives a personal description of the city, the people and the problems as he found them. Winthrop, a product of St. Mark's and Harvard, who with Gen Norstad's Atlantic Council of the United States in Washington, is on a world pleasure trip with Deborah, his bride of four months.

WINTHROP

The 3.5-hour flight to Saigon was routine and tedious until we reached the coast of Viet Nam. This final hour of the trip was a visual feast.

Expansive beaches of pure white sand greeted us as we came in from the South China Sea. The occupied village, along with the green mountains rolling inland, were enshrouded in a series of the most spectacular cloud formations we had ever seen. With the setting sun on our right, we flew southward over the lowlands, the rice paddies, and strategic hamlets. We even saw a series of fires which we were told later were probably the result of fighting.

We were met at the airport by a transplanted Frenchman who married a Vietnamese girl seven years ago and who is now the manager of the Saigon branch of a United States insurance firm. They drove us to the Caravelle Hotel and bade us farewell until the following evening at which time we were to be their guests for dinner.

Early Monday morning we embarked on the tour of Saigon. This was to be our only full day in the Republic of Viet Nam's capital, now the center of so much attention. Our guide was a boy of 20 who introduced himself as John: "But why don't you call me Jack!" – so we did.

Lush, Peaceful

We climbed into our car on the fashionable To Do St. and took a quick look at the government building and the Abraham Lincoln Library. We then went across town to the Botant Garden which is a lush and peaceful park in the middle of this busy city. Among the green lawns, and tidy gardens, small zoo and happy children, we found it hard to believe that we were actually in Saigon – the city where battles are being launched against the Viet Cong and where Buddhist monks burn themselves alive in protest against Diem's religious intolerance.

Only a few blocks away we visited the main Buddhist pagoda where crowds were forming to demonstrate. Protest signs in three languages, stating that the U. S. is responsible for protecting and supporting the Buddhist cause, were draped across the entrance to the temple. Jack warned us against going in, so we took a photograph from the outside and listened to the weird flute music playing within.

We returned to the car and pushed on, through a maze of bicycles, to another Buddhist temple where people were gathering for their morning worship.

We nodded greetings to a monk and wondered whether tomorrow morning would bring with it another Buddhist sacrifice. Jack took us to the spot where the monk had burned himself recently. Wide boulevards of the city provided the more scenic side to our tour. The women's pastel silk dresses, billowing out around their white satin pants and revealing tiny waists, were far more elegant than the Chinese costumes. But the bicycles give the city most of its character. It is estimated that today there are 200,000 bicycles in Saigon (hence its nick name: "City on Wheels").

We also went to Cholon, which in 1954 became part of Saigon. Cholon is the Chinese part of town, and here the Chinese population is approximately 300,000. In Cholon we became involved in an interesting conversation with Jack.

Like U. S. Negroes

Jack opened the gate to a discussion by saying that he was Chinese and there in Saigon the Chinese were very much like the Negroes in America. It turned out that he was the Youngest child in his family and

the only one born outside of China – his family having fled to Viet Nam just before the Communist takeover.

He was fascinated by the prejudice toward the Negro minority in the United States and, like so many, had a distorted picture of the facts – he had read all about the unjust incidents but nothing of the improvements.

Jack said that American films have been very popular in Saigon and particularly those focusing on the Negro-White problem. "Chained," a film about a black man and a white man's escape from prison, lasted many months; and "Imitation of Life," based on an illegitimate white girl's hatred toward her Negro mother, was the most popular film in Saigon this year. Jack's sympathy was obviously with the Negro mother. ("It was very sad, very sad.")

In contrast, the American award-winner "Ben Hur" lasted only a week or so. Jack spoke of Marlon Brando's support of the Negro demonstrations in America and we asked if he had seen Brando's performance in "The Ugly American" (filed in Viet Nam). Jack said no, that he had only read about Brando in the newspaper, for "The Ugly American" was barred in Viet Nam. The Viet Nam government apparently believed the movie to be both anti-Communist and anti-Viet Nam (a sorry state of affairs, indeed.)

Jack was frank about the typical American tourists. He said that he had been with the travel agency only a short time and was trying his best, but the group of Americans he had led the day before neither took his advice nor listened to his explanations.

Our overall impression of Jack was unquestionably favorable. He was extremely eager to be helpful and polite and revealed an almost childlike need to be understood.

He was a person confused by many of the forces at work in his rapidly changing world (his sympathies are with the Buddhists in the current struggle, yet he wants to rid his country of the Viet Cong). When we left him at noon-time, we wished him "good luck," and meant it.

Guide's Ideas

Dinner with our guides was very pleasant. We went to a night cub adjoining the hotel for dinner. Here we saw a floor show which featured a superb magician, Filipino dancers, and a Vietnamese singer. Our guide gave us his ideas on several subjects:

As a Frenchman who had lived in Viet Nam since World War II, he said he now considered this country his home, but he felt that the United States was fighting a losing battle here, and should pull out. A guerilla war such as this cannot be won, he said. Furthermore, he felt, Diem's government was thoroughly corrupt and, although a Catholic himself, said that the government had been rumored to bribe Buddhist peasants with rice to add to the Catholic following in Viet Nam. (Diem's brother is now an archbishop.) Such practices can only lead to increasing trouble, he said.

As for the business outlook, he felt that things were indeed uncertain and that Diem's policies did not give ground for optimism. He indicated that his own branch office was having difficulties at the present time.

One additional observation of our guide deserves comment. He said that in Cambodia the up-and-coming young men in the government show very little evidence of such corruption, injustice, and confusion, and in contrast they are devout communists!

This is a bad omen for Southeast Asia, he said. The same thought was echoed by another recently-made friend, an American, who said with some emotion that the United States always seems to be backed into the unhappy position of supporting the most unpopular and "rightist" losers. He cited Batista, Chiang Kai-shek and Diem as examples.

The evening's entertainment ended at midnight and we retired quite exhausted by a long and informative day.

The next day our guide put the final touch on his hospitality by giving us a ride to the airport. En route he continued his pessimistic appraisal of the present situation in South Viet Nam.

He said that before going to bed many nights he could hear shelling against the Viet Cong only 10 miles outside the city. He went on to say that such violence barely alarmed him any more so long as he was near his family.

At the airport we noticed considerable activity. Several helicopters drifted by overhead and there were troops in the terminal.

The Boston Globe

Monday, September 2, 1963

Far East Diary II
'A New Type of Bomb'

John Winthrop and Deborah, his bride of four months, set out on a world trip from Boston last June. They are still abroad … and keeping a diary. In yesterday's *Sunday Globe*, Winthrop – a product of St. Mark's and Harvard, and now on the staff of Gen Norstad's Atlantic Council of the United States in Washington – told of their visit to embattled Viet Nam. Today, the *Globe* starts printing a few pages of his diary, begun as the couple flew by way of Hawaii to Japan and then on around the world.

WINTHROP

KYOTO, Japan, July 2 – Our final evening here was spent on an after-dinner excursion to see the widely-talked-about cormorant fisherman. This unique method of fishing is not entirely pleasant to see – particularly after a full meal.

The fishing boat, with a crew of three men, drifts along the water at night.

A fire is built in a wire basket which is extended over the water, and six cormorants scoot about beneath the fire to catch the fish. The fish, however, cannot be swallowed by the birds who have metal rings around their necks. The cormorants are controlled by a crew member who has each by a short leash.

They are encouraged to catch fish by a low warbling sound which the members of the crew make continually. When the fish are attracted by the light and semi-swallowed by the birds, the cormorants are yanked into the boat and their throats are squeezed, forcing them to give up their catch.

This method has been employed by Kyoto fisherman for centuries.

★

July 3 – Deb and I arose early for the long automobile trip to Osaka via Nara, the ancient capital of Japan.

Nagasaka, a Japanese man of my age, was to be our guide for the day.

He is a graduate student (Japanese literature) at Kyoto University. His English is almost perfect. We learned in the course of our conversation that his father went to Amherst and that his entire family is strongly westernized.

At the time of the dropping of the atomic bomb, Nagasaka was living outside Hiroshima, since his father was a professor at the University of Hiroshima.

Nagasaka said he remembered the day when he was in grade school and heard the blast of the bomb seconds after seeing the blinding light. Windows were broken in the school but no one was hurt.

The students were told simply that "a new type of bomb had been exploded" and sent home.

It was two weeks before Nagasaka learned that his father had not gone to the university on that fatal morning but had taken the day off from his work to do research in another town.

★

Deb managed to get a lot of information out of Nagasaka on the subject of Japanese marriages.

Apparently 70 percent of Japanese marriages today are still arranged by the parents; only 1 or 2 percent of these marriages end in failure.

A go-between (generally a friend of the family) often suggests the match and officiates in the exchange of pictures. Meetings are then arranged among the two families. The young pair are generally included and left alone to talk afterwards.

This arranged courtship lasts a maximum of six months before the wedding ceremony. Ten to 15 percent of the Western style marriages end in divorce in this country.

Nagasaka said that he still preferred the type of marriage where the partners made the choice.

★

In the afternoon we visited Dreamland, Japan's answer to Disneyland. This delightful city of amusements and fantasy for children is bigger and better than our effort.

It took us 1.5 hours to roam through the grounds and take a few pictures. The theme was strongly Old West throughout. There was an American Indian encampment, an old mining tour village and a shooting arcade for Japanese children who want to play cowboy.

At one point we were approached timidly by a Japanese father who had bought his son a Hopalong Cassidy cap pistol. He wanted to take our picture standing beside his son.

Just after we cheerfully agreed, the small boy looked up at us and fled in tears, refusing to cooperate. We obviously terrified him.

NEXT: A pilgrimage to Hiroshima, "A dwelling place for the conscience of the world."

Tuesday, September 3, 1963

Far East Diary-III
Book of 200,000 Names

HIROSHIMA, July 5 and 6 – Today we embarked on a hastily arranged pilgrimage to Hiroshima. It somehow seemed appropriate to visit this rebuilt city after our trip to Pearl Harbor. There is no question that our trip to Hiroshima, which lasted the 5th and 6th of July and included long train trips to and from Osaka, will remain a vivid memory for both Deborah and myself. While by no means the most pleasant part of our visit in Japan, our trip to Hiroshima gave us a small clue in understanding the people in this country of contrasts.

WINTHROP

We arrived at 2:00 in the afternoon. The sky was heavily overcast and a slow drizzle was soaking the city's wide boulevards. Despite the rain, we decided to see the city before settling down in our inn.

Our first destination was Hijiyama, a hill from which one can get a panoramic view of Hiroshima.

It is also the location for the laboratory where United States and Japanese scientists work to jointly and persistently in studying the effects of the bomb (roughly 40 people still die annually from radioactivity and related causes).

From this hill we could see that Hiroshima is nestled among steep mountains and divided by a wide river.

From this hill also we could vaguely appreciate the extent of damage caused by the atomic blast on the morning of August 8, 1945. (There was nearly total destruction within 1.5 miles of epicenter and widespread damage beyond.)

★

It was not until we reached the Peace Memorial and the museum, however, that we could really understand why Hiroshima has been called "a dwelling place for the conscience of the world."

Here, in the middle of Hiroshima, one is surrounded by new buildings and a city rebuilt. The shell of the old industrial exhibition hall remains as the sole grim reminder of the bomb.

Less than a mile from it lies the modernistic museum-hotel-auditorium and between the two (in a perfect line) lies the memorial shrine.

This shrine is simply a marble tablet

beneath a small archway. On the tablet is inscribed in Japanese:

"Rest in Peace;
We shall not make this mistake again."

And hidden beneath it lies a notebook containing the names of all the identifiable victims (more than 200,000) of the atomic bomb. In front of the shrine lay some wet flowers.

★

Here in the cold drizzle Deborah and I stood for a few minutes. Several nondescript Japanese came up the pathway to the shrine, looked at us, went up in front of the flowers to pay their respects, then looked at us again and departed.

The museum consisted of little more than graphic reminders of the horror of the bomb. The visitor learns why another war must never come, if he did not know this already.

As the only Americans in the crowded display room we were both happy to leave.

NEXT: Formosa, where the Free Chinese consider themselves as people in transit, only temporary inhabitants before winning back their homeland.

The Boston Globe

Wednesday, September 4, 1963

Far East Diary-IV

Free China's Vincent Su

TAIPEI, Formosa, July 12 – Our arrival in Taipei was a nightmare. We found ourselves standing in the middle of an enormous line moving at a snail's pace toward the passport-customs desk. This wait was made doubly unpleasant by the tropical heat which had hit us like a breath from an oven as soon as we had emerged from the air-conditioned airplane.

We were approached by a sturdy Chinese fellow of about my age who handed me two cards, one of a Vincent Su and the other of a Wilken Shen. As he handed me the cards he

WINTHROP

said in flawless English, "My name is Vincent Su; call me 'Vincent'. I'll be waiting for you to get your bags and take you to your hotel."

Our hotel turned out to be a palace. Modeled after the Imperial Palace in Peking and completed in May of this year, Taipei's Grand Hotel has already been visited by the king and queen of Thailand. The interior was extravagant in the extreme. From the huge marble staircase to the decorated ceilings and ornamental jade displays, it was and is an air-conditioned island in the sun. (We highly recommend it to anyone visiting Taiwan.)

In the afternoon we went on a brief sightseeing trip outside the city with Vincent. We saw the lush and beautiful Yangmingshan National Park in the mountains beyond Chiang Kai-shek's home.

★

July 13 – The National Historical Museum, the Presidential Square and the government offices were predictably unexciting.

I say predictably only because it soon became obvious to me why any nationalistic showpiece in Formosa does not have the meaning that such points of interest have in most countries. The Chiang or Free China people now living in Formosa regard themselves as people in transit – or temporary inhabitants of this island nation.

This fact became more and more obvious in our discussions with Vincent.

★

July 14 – I will paraphrase Vincent's comments on several items:

On the return to the mainland – It is inevitable because of the widespread discontent on the mainland now. The people of Free China will not mind fighting their relatives; this is one of life's many hardships. Besides, most are beginning to forget their families now.

On war – It is all we have known; we are not afraid of it. (Vincent is a hard-bitten soldier, as his ideas may reveal. He is at present a reserve officer in the army. He remembers the Japanese invasion as a child; he fled the mainland at the age of 18; he fought in the Korean conflict as one of 300 volunteers from Free China; and he survived the shelling of Quemoy when he served there in his own army.)

On the United States and its leaders – Strongly pro United States. Unlike Great Britain, we have always stood behind them. Eisenhower, as a personal friend of the Generalissimo, was a great favorite here. Democrats are not quite as popular as Republicans. A "wait and see" attitude toward the Kennedy administration prevails, to some extent, but the climate is and always has been pro United States.

On marriage – Only Western style marriages exist here in Taiwan, i.e. arranged by the participants and not the parents. You rarely find mixed marriages between the Taiwanese and these who have recently come from China.

On the Taiwanese – A bit gaudy in their taste but harmless. Not much resentment is felt toward the more recent inhabitants.

★

The more we got to know Vincent the more we began to realize that he lived in a world of black and white with little of the grey, little room for compromise.

NEXT: Hong Kong, where one actually rubs shoulders with Red Chinese and their brand of Communism.

The Boston Globe

Thursday, September 5, 1963

Far East Diary-V

Dragon in Hong Kong

HONG KONG, July 28 – Deborah and I had several glimpses of the flag of Red China (red with white stars in the upper left corner). The third day we were in Hong Kong we went down to the docks to see the Communist vessels unloading goods from "the Mainland." The carriers became highly irritated when we took their pictures. (A friend later explained to us that they were merely superstitious old Chinese who thought a reflecting mechanism in the camera turned them upside down.)

WINTHROP

Another day we saw more of the same type of activity when we went on an all day boat ride with some newly made American friends, the Allmans and the Iertons.

Again we saw the flag and the influence of Red China in a somewhat more threatening way when we passed the commencement exercises of a Communist boys school being held outdoors. Pictures of Mao and Chou En-lai were conspicuously displayed along with Chinese Communist flags – nothing Russian as the Sino-Soviet split has just become irrevocable. (I took one hurried picture and pray it comes out!)

"These schools are cheaper and cater to the poor," said a friend, 'But there are only four of them in Hong Kong."

When we thought about it, we were amazed there were not more.

★

Our final look at the "Chinese dragon" came on an afternoon excursion to Macau. We flew down in a twin engine sea plane, which held only the two of us, two additional passengers and a thoroughly competent and genial British pilot. The trip lasted only 15 minutes but it was exciting and great fun.

Macau itself was anticlimactic.

It was teaming hot when we arrived at 3:30 in the afternoon, and the two-hour tour we squeezed in before the evening ferry ride back to Hong Kong was made doubly unpleasant by a guide and a cab driver who tried to cheat us.

Aside from a good view of the border, where Portuguese and Red Chinese confront each other, we also saw an old Portuguese fort, which commanded a superb view of the city, and an old graveyard which had become famous because of American and

107

British seamen (of the East India Trading Co.) buried there. We also visited the gambling casino and took a ride over the cobble stoned streets in a rickshaw.

★

"Hong Kong is a city of contrasts."

This has been said so many times that is sounds like a childish observation and yet there can be few places where the statement is as appropriate.

At one moment the visitor is climbing out of a jet plane; the next he is looking at rickshaws.

After riding the escalator in the ultra-modern Hong Kong Hilton, he can walk a few steps and see apartment buildings where the rooms accommodate an average of six inhabitants.

The contrasts are endless: Grinding poverty vs. luxurious modern efficiency; East vs. West – they are all here in Hong Kong.

Our stay at "Lookout" gave Deborah and me a look at one side of life in this city – the very best.

Having learned that we have been preceded by such notable guests as Attorney General Robert Kennedy, the David Rockefellers, former Vice President Richard Nixon and others, we now understand why "Lookout" has attracted these and other famous citizens from around the world.

The drive from the airport took nearly an hour. We crossed on the ferry to Victoria and then swooped up the mountain road above the city, marveling at the panoramic views each turn brought with it.

Finally, we turned an unexpected left and tore up a narrow driveway. As we rounded the last turn, a white Spanish-styled villa rose before us – this was "Lookout."

We had no sooner been ushered to the air-conditioned interior of the villa than we realized how "Lookout" got its name: At the far end of the central room on the ground floor was a huge picture window which revealed a spectacular view framed in the white archway of the front terrace. We were high on a hill overlooking the ocean – the green cliffs tumbling several hundred feet to the water's edge.

★

Hong Kong's other side does not inspire long-winded description.

But despite mortifying living conditions, the inhabitants of Hong Kong do not appear desperate. At all times of day we have passed through Victoria's busy streets and seen people sleeping on the sidewalk, because they do not have room in their homes. We have seen some people hunting for scraps of food, and we have seen others with terrible afflictions.

But they all seem happy.

The Boston Globe

Saturday, September 7, 1963

Far East Diary-VII
A Face in Calcutta

CALCUTTA, India, Aug. 12 – Calcutta has 6.5 million people and is the largest city in the world's largest democracy. Calcutta is also a "hell-hole." The most casual visitor cannot help emotionally coming to grips with the stark, hard realities of this city.

I watched a young boy carrying what looked like a dog dish on one of the streets near the hotel. He saw me leaning against a building with my camera and absorbing the scenery about me. He approached me for a better look and stopped

WINTHROP

several yards away. He was dressed in a dirty white shirt and gray shorts – no shoes. His face reflected the cruelties life had shown him, but it also reflected hope and character. The boy did not beg although the clothes and dish may have been all he owned.

After a good look he walked away – stealing glances at me over his shoulder until he disappeared behind a wall.

It occurred to me afterwards that this 5 or 6-year-old boy, whose face will haunt me for a long time, symbolized Calcutta and, in a broader sense, India herself.

He was struggling to establish his independence in a world with seemed remote indeed from America. His needs were many and his future was uncertain and yet he had hope and pride.

★

As we approached the heart of Calcutta we passed oxen pulling coal, and cows lying along the streets amidst thousands and thousands of people. The city was hard at work in the semi-darkness – carrying, building, walking, running, sweating.

Waves of heavy heat and foul odors poured into the car from the clogged streets.

A beggar came to the car window at one street crossing. At another intersection there was a violent screech of brakes as a car speeding in the opposite direction hit a pedestrian.

We toured Calcutta with an Indian who had his law degree, but who worked for the travel agency because the pay there ($3 per day) was better than any job he could get elsewhere. Our tour was complete and informative.

Two sights, in particular, we will not forget: One, a bare-breasted mother waking

109

up on the pavement to feed her crying baby; another, a young boy squatting on the sidewalk as he picked lice out of an old man's scalp.

We had seen evidence of progress made here in recent years, but the problems that remained seemed so enormous.

★

Kashmir, Aug. 18 – The air in Kashmir is pure and soft and was a refreshing contrast to Bangkok, Calcutta and Delhi. As we waited for our half-asleep travel agent to get us to our hotel, this was the first impression we had – the wonderful smell of this cool, soft air.

A boat trip on Dahl Lake carried us through myriad floating lotus flowers and lily pads. Deb and I had great fun skimming beads of water across the oily surface of the lily pads as the drops glinted like tiny molecules of mercury in the bright sunlight. As we were paddled through the tall marshes and wooded areas, we suddenly came upon floating vegetable gardens and small islands. Our boatman stopped at one garden and climbed aboard to show us how the gardens would sink and then surface again, and we were handed sun-ripened tomatoes, melons and corn.

We passed several native wooden houses on these floating islands with chickens and pigs running in and out of the house and children swimming and playing at the water's edge.

★

Kashmir has introduced us to one of the most spectacular parts of the world (and I have exhausted my list of superlatives in trying to describe it.)

END OF SERIES

World Away

John Winthrop takes his son, Grenville, on a memorable Audubon trip to Alaska, complete with grizzlies, moose, salmon fishing and mountains.

It has been said that Alaska is a land of contrasts and it surely is. This summer my twelve-year-old son, Grenville, and I took a hurried but memorable trip together from Seattle to Juneau to Anchorage to Mount McKinley to Glacier Bay. The contrast in weather alone set the pace. Traveling by car, boat, plane and train within a single week, we were alternately warmed by the sun and drenched in the rain. Through the mountain passes, on the way to view Mount McKinley, we were fog bound and frozen by hail. Within a short period of time the sky cleared and we were able to see the tallest mountain on the continent, forty miles away, drenched in sunlight.

Contrast in topography itself was equally dramatic. The jagged edges of the Alaska range and the flat tundra, the spruce woods of the moose and the elevated, treeless home of the Dal sheep, the vast rivers and cascading waterfalls – all serve to punctuate the variety as well as the natural beauty of the state.

JOHN WINTHROP
His trip to Alaska was part of a project of the National Audubon Society to preserve wilderness for posterity. Winthrop is chairman and chief executive officer of Wood, Struthers and Winthrop, a New York-based financial service. He is a descendant and namesake of the first governor of Massachusetts and the first governor of Connecticut.

A Wilderness Society

The attitudes and people provided another dimension to the contrasts. My son and I were part of an Ad Hoc Committee of the National Audubon Society in favor of preserving the wilderness for posterity. As such, we were exposed to far more briefings and introduced to more Alaskan natives than one would normally expect. We met the developers and the environmentalists, the Indians and the Eskimos, the transplants and the escapists, the students and the teachers, along with political aspirants. All viewpoints were represented among the sparsely populated civilization in Alaska. It's a wilderness society, however; the feeling that the State must be in control of its own destiny prevails.

Some Impressions

In addition to the contrasts, my son and I left Alaska with some impressions and memories.

– A tour of Juneau with an Audubon volunteer who took us on a picnic by a stream outside the city where salmon spawned.

– A session with Governor Hammond who talked about the wilderness issue. His efforts to straddle the positions of the developers and the environmentalists was of less than consuming interest to Gren, but he learned from listening.

– The spectacle of a grizzly bear crossing a stream with two young cubs. Our driver helped notify a lone hiker who was in their path about the advancing danger.

– A moose appearing as we walked toward our hotel in the mountains one evening. We gave her a wide berth.

– Interesting conversations with natives on television and at the University of Alaska. Gradually, it became obvious that people in a frontier society were more cordial and less threatened. People wave to one another as they pass on the road.

– A fishing expedition allowing us to make contact with the creatures of the deep as we bagged a thirty-five pound king salmon and a good sized kelp in Glacier Bay.

– A boat trip through blue icebergs alongside massive cliffs and snow capped peaks bringing us near the home of seals and a thousand birds.

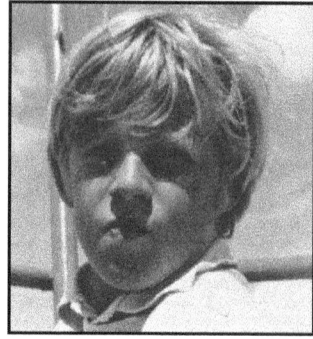

GRENVILLE WINTHROP

"Almost Spiritual"

If none of the above convinced us that the spectacular beauty of Alaska must be preserved for our children and grandchildren, the flight by Mount McKinley did. We crowded into a small plane at midnight on June 21st with the setting sun on one side of the sky and the moon on the other. Alongside the massive topographical wonder, we flew in silence. The experience was almost spiritual; the memory unforgettable – no clouds, snowcapped peaks as far as the eye could see.

The adventure did not end alone with these memories but rather with the overall tone of Alaska which is set by the wilderness. The wildlife in all its varied forms along with the majesty of the wilderness itself dominates the experience. A final note: if any father has the opportunity to share all of this with his son, he should take it.

-JOHN WINTHROP

September 1978

Denali - Home of the Sun

The "almost spiritual experience" of an airborne view of Mt. McKinley
as recounted by John Winthrop

The view from the summit of Mount McKinley has been compared to that seen from a window of heaven. The Indians called the mountain "Denali", ("the high one") and believed it was the home of the sun. I prefer that name; it seems less dollar-studded, more timeless, more appropriate. Today, many visitors come to Mount McKinley National Park — particularly in the warmer months — and find the main spectacle enshrouded in clouds. They send home postcards of the mountain without having seen it and enjoy viewing the enormous variety of wildlife in the park.

But those who actually see this famous mountain are left with an experience they will never forget. It is massive and splendid; it is forbidding and awesome. It is more than the dominant topographical spectacle in the State. Denali has an element of spiritual dominance as well. Some want to climb it every year. They are captivated by it — perhaps even hypnotized by it — and a few make the ultimate sacrifice in trying to scale its treacherous flanks.

Many want to view it from the park and will travel by bus for miles to do so. A few want to fly up to it — skimming along the valley and tearing through the mountain passes with audacity and, then, drinking in the view from many angles. To me, that is the berries. And to do this with one of my sons, Grenville by name was an experience I cannot forget.

Grizzlies, Moose

We had put in a full day in the park recording our encounters with seven grizzlies, eight moose, 120 Dal sheep, two herds of caribou and a wide variety of birds and other wildlife. Conditions were good, but not ideal for viewing the largest mountain in North America. Once we returned to the hotel, the cloud cover lifted quite dramatically, however, and by suppertime conditions were ideal for an overflight.

Gren and I arrived at the airport at 11:45 p.m. A full moon had crept over the mountains near the hotel airport and splashes of crimson decorated the other end of the heavens. Overhead the sky remained cloudless and light blue — never to darken now that it was late June in the year. A group of six of us climbed into a Piper, gratified by the ideal conditions and excited by the prospect ahead.

By 12:10, we had fueled the aircraft, taxied down the runway and were taking off toward the midnight sun. We climbed rapidly and steeply, finally leveling off above the tree line. Almost immediately the urge to take pictures was with us. The moon shrank in size as the setting sun became more prominent. Once we were level with the lesser mountains in the Alaska Range, we could tell that a recent snow had dusted the peaks and given all of them a crisp elegance as far as the eye could see. In all directions the mountains spread capped by snow and reaching into the darker regions below. Dead ahead lay Denali — too far to view at first.

Our altitude climbed imperceptibly to 7,000 and to 8,000 feet. Nearly all the mountain tops were below us then. The scenery improved as we drifted over close to several peaks — so close the wing tips almost seemed to touch the white snow. Several times we were treated to the breathtaking thrill of climbing alongside a new slope, then seeing the earth fall away in a sudden cliff. The unexpected caverns, the jagged edges, the graceful slopes up and down the valleys made us want to freeze the moment on film. Knowing we couldn't duplicate the experience adequately, Gren and I tried anyway — snapping pictures from time to time as we bucked a strong headwind up the valley.

Gradually we approached the objective. Rising like a gigantic humpback whale ahead of us, the mountain dwarfed all the peaks for miles around; one could only be overwhelmed. Clearly, we would be unable to fly at the level of its peak, which rose over 20,000 feet above sea level. Ahead of us it lay glowing in the midnight sun — massive and dominant. Our aircraft seemed like a mechanical toy as we approached halfway up its base. Gusts of high winds picked up snow in the higher regions and sent it spiraling off the mountain's surface at crazy angles. The moon hovered over the scene — a splendid, shining sphere. The sun —

temporarily submerged under the horizon as the time approached 1:00 a.m. — still made its presence evident.

As we coasted around the edge of Denali, there was clearly enough light to spot climbers and even to take pictures. While awesome by any measurement, the primary impression of the moment was one of peace. There was a timeless quality which this particular mountain seemed to offer more than any I had seen. The dominance was absolute. We crept along the edge — all of us in silence — occasionally taking pictures, but mostly just coasting with the changing beauty — diminished and enhanced simultaneously by the experience.

Soon it was over. We had made it to the outer limit, banked steeply and were heading back to the airstrip. The purr of the airplane engine seemed to take on a different tone. A strong tail wind picked up our ground speed. Soon Denali was behind us and we could talk once more without feeling irreverent. While it was difficult to communicate in any detail our reactions, my son and I knew we had shared a very rare experience. When we left the airplane together, he thanked me for it. I should have thanked him. If we didn't look out the window of heaven together, we came mighty close to it. And, I may not have made the trip, if he had not been with me.

JOHN WINTHROP
JULY 1978

THE
GREENWICH
REVIEW

date unknown

A South American Journal

Some months ago John Winthrop took leave for a year from the chairmanship of his New York firm, Wood, Struthers & Winthrop Management Company, in order to work for the political campaign of George H. W. Bush. At the same time, he sat down with a pad and pencil to compile a list of lesser projects for the same period. "Far and away the most glamorous of these," he relates, "was the fulfillment of a long-standing dream to visit South America, a fascinating part

Author at Inca ruins above Cuzco.

of the world – with tremendous natural resources – and one about which we have compelling reasons to educate ourselves." To businessman-historian-conservationist Winthrop, his two weeks' itinerary last autumn seemed a natural progression through the historical-cultural development of that continent as well as its advancing economic evolution and brilliant prospects; from Peru, ancient center of the Incas, to Argentina, business hub of today, and Brazil, with all its promise for tomorrow. In this issue and the next, *The Greenwich Review* reprints with permission excerpts from "A South American Journal."

The Valdez Peninsula, Argentina
November 4, 1979

Ballena means whale in Spanish; the Argentines pronounce it "Bajena." Along the Valdez Peninsula, Argentina has some of the most extraordinary whaling waters in the world. This same area also contains some of the most spectacular marine habitat located anywhere – most famous perhaps for the elephant seal breeding grounds.

Penguins and a wide variety of sea birds grace the shores of this arid peninsula, but seeing the ballena was to be the main focus for a memorable weekend adventure with a small group of Argentine friends.

The sky was cloudless as we awoke on the morning of November 4. The Argentines don't make much of a fuss over breakfast. Lunch and dinner are the big meals. So, I joined our group for orange juice, toast and

tea. When I was halfway through the cup of tea, whales were sighted in the bay just outside our hotel. We tore outside, picking up cameras, boots and jackets. Two yellow rubber boats were already in the water with Johnson outboard motors firmly in place. We divided ourselves into two groups and climbed aboard.

The water was calm and unbelievably clear in the bay. As we sped toward the spouting whales, we could see the ocean bottom sliding beneath us, Not a person could be seen on the beach or along the cliffs, which tumbled to the water's edge on either side of the bay. Only a small group of the deer-like guanacos could be seen high on one cliff silhouetted against the blue sky. The setting was stark, clear – almost primeval.

I was absorbed by the haunting beauty when the water broke one hundred yards away in front of us and a barnacled right whale spouted indifferently as he rolled over. We cut our engine and drifted toward the spot. For a period of time, nothing happened. No noise. No motion. No whale. Then the world around us exploded, as the enormous animal surfaced to our side. He turned and headed directly for our boat.

When a man confronts a whale in this manner, he is reminded not of his inadequacy so much as of his total helplessness. In this sense, everything snapped into perspective, as the huge mountain of gray rolled toward me. The back, a darker gray, rose high out of the water and then down – following the head under our tiny rubber boat. Finally, the tail disappeared beneath us. One could only pray as the massive body drifted under the boat. A small twist of the tail could turn us over into the icy waters as he became playful. Again and again, he glided around us, under us and between the boats.

Two times we were actually nudged by our giant friend – both times gentle taps with the tail. Soon, he was joined by a second whale, which had been rolling and spouting through the waters some distance away. For a few somewhat terrifying but glorious moments, these two creatures of the deep played around us together. Finally, they drifted off to their own mysterious world, leaving all of us spellbound – even bereft – for we had gradually become used to them and almost made friends. If we had been merely committed to saving the whales before this incident, all of us were now passionate advocates.

An Argentine friend captured the experience well by saying that it was almost as if the whale was trying to communicate with us. "I am big, but I am also gentle and friendly and playful." Each wanted to give us this message it seemed.

I left the beach wishing all mankind could have been in that raft with us, and made a new friend in such a spectacular way.

Oddly enough, the rest of the day was not anticlimactic. We went to an island inhabited by guanacos (best described as a cross between a white-tailed deer and a camel.) On the edge of the island, we were free to roam on the smooth, pebbled beaches

LEFT: A barnacled right whale surfaces beside the tiny boat as it drifts silently with the engine cut.

RIGHT: Submerging just enough to skim underneath, the whale surfaces immediately on the other side of the boat.

and walk up to the drowsy elephantine seals. The penguins too let us get very close to them. Only the guanacos, curious but suspicious, remained at a safe distance.

We had a feast of roasted lamb, cheese, tomatoes and wine. Then we went south along the peninsula in the afternoon. The wildlife variety should be recorded in far more detail than time permits. Among the birds were unusual species of hawks, owls and partridge; also, a pair of beautiful Antarctic doves.

We stopped high atop a cliff, spending nearly an hour viewing the rambunctious sea lions far below, their cries of play and anger echoing loudly against the cliff walls.

A thousand seabirds swirled below us. White caps covered the dark blue ocean.

The sky was so clear that one almost felt, looking south against a brisk wind, that it would be possible to see Antarctica. I was informed, however, that it was nearly three thousand miles away. Such a scene is difficult to leave – desolate but captivating in its beauty – a festival of bird and marine activity.

THE
GREENWICH
REVIEW

date unknown

A South American Journal

Last month. *The Greenwich Review* presented Greenwich resident John Winthrop's description of his visit to the Valdez Peninsula in Argentina to observe its teeming wildlife and, in particular, the giant right whales of the region from the close-up vantage point of a tiny rubber boat. This was part of a brief South American tour undertaken by the author last autumn while on leave from the chairmanship of Wood, Struthers & Winthrop Management Company in New York City, prior to working for the George Bush political campaign. From the same trip, The Review presents, with permission, further excerpts from "A South American Journal."

Cuzco, Peru
October 31, 1979

Cuzco's outskirts are blemished with tragic evidences of poverty. Mud huts, overgrazed hillsides, donkeys and cows and chickens, open sewers and sad, sad faces – particularly among the children—all combine to form a confused picture of despair until the train gets away from the city. Then, the majesty of the farmland and mountains overcomes the evidence of poverty.

November is springtime in Peru. It should be the season of planting and building and hope, but the poverty of this beautiful country smothers hope and creates a lasting

The ubiquitous llamas graze among remnants of a civilization that once dominated the continent. Among the docile animals, a Peruvian boy overlooks the striking contrasts of past glory and present poverty is his native land with the indifference of everyday familiarity.

impression on almost any visitor.

The extraordinary spectacle of

Machu Picchu lived up to all expectations, however. Located on the outer fringes of the Amazon jungle and perched high in the mountains 8,000 feet above sea level, Machu Picchu attracts well over 100,000 visitors from all corners of the world every year. The bus trip up the mountainside through the hair pin turns is a bit unsettling, but soon one arrives at the Inca ruins and begins the journey back into time.

Very little is known about the industrious, talented people who actually made these remarkable terraced walls and monuments during the thirteenth century. The functional areas of the five and one-half square miles appear to be pretty well identified— the living quarters of the royalty, the intellectuals, and the workers. A large sundial testifies to the awareness of the heavens, geography, and time. The lookouts are studies in spectacular as well as courageous building skill as

Fifty miles from Cuzco, Machu Picchu dominates the surrounding countryside from its spectacular mountain-top site, as this great fortress city once commanded the heights of Inca civilization.

A bus plies the steep mountain trail with its precarious hairpin turn, between lofty Machu Picchu and the rural station of the train for CMXO far below. This "modern" transportation system (much more than the world famed Inca ruins) is the main attraction for local children who flock about hoping for a handout from the tourists.

"Sacsahuamán, meaning satisfied eagle to the ancient Incas, and often referred to as the Temple of the Sun by English speaking visitors, is located high above Cuzco in Peru at an altitude of 12,000 feet," explains John Winthrop. "Before I left for South America, a good friend said; 'Don't miss it.' He was right. Visiting the Temple of the Sun is an experience one is not likely to forget.

"On both sides of the elevated, grassy plateau overlooking Cuzco are constructions of massive stones – painstakingly shaped centuries ago and then placed next to each other and on top of one another in the shape of a zigzag fortress or walls. Perhaps the most remarkable feature of these monuments of the past is the way in which these enormous stones fit next to each other – with such precision and care that I could remember no construction that compared to it. "Many of the stones were removed by the Spanish invaders. The remnants are still splendid beyond description. I wanted to remain among these ruins alone with the llamas grazing nearby. The altitude produces a good dose of lethargy, and perhaps contributed to my feeling that nothing of consequence was happening beyond this peaceful scene."

of peace and timelessness as well. It is only the clusters of tourists making noise and leaving litter that break the spell. Even the beautiful wild flowers, growing among the stonework, were picked by some of the careless visitors. After three hours it was over. We boarded buses once again and headed down the mountainside to the train station.

A small, barefoot boy, no more than ten years old, ran down the face of the mountain and intercepted our bus, waving goodbye to the passengers after each sweeping zigzag turn. He met us by the railroad station, after running the full distance of the twenty minute trip, and held out his hand as we got off the bus – hoping for tangible approval. The contrast between the majesty of the past and the misery of the present – symbolized by this exhausted small boy – was tough to escape as I reached into my pocket to reward him for his heroic effort to please us.

they are perched on cliffs in most cases. The agricultural techniques appear to have been remarkably advanced. But, many details are missing. So little is known about the history of these people.

The twentieth century visitor can only be left awed by the wonder of this kingdom high in the mountains. Wandering alone among the ruins I could not escape feelings

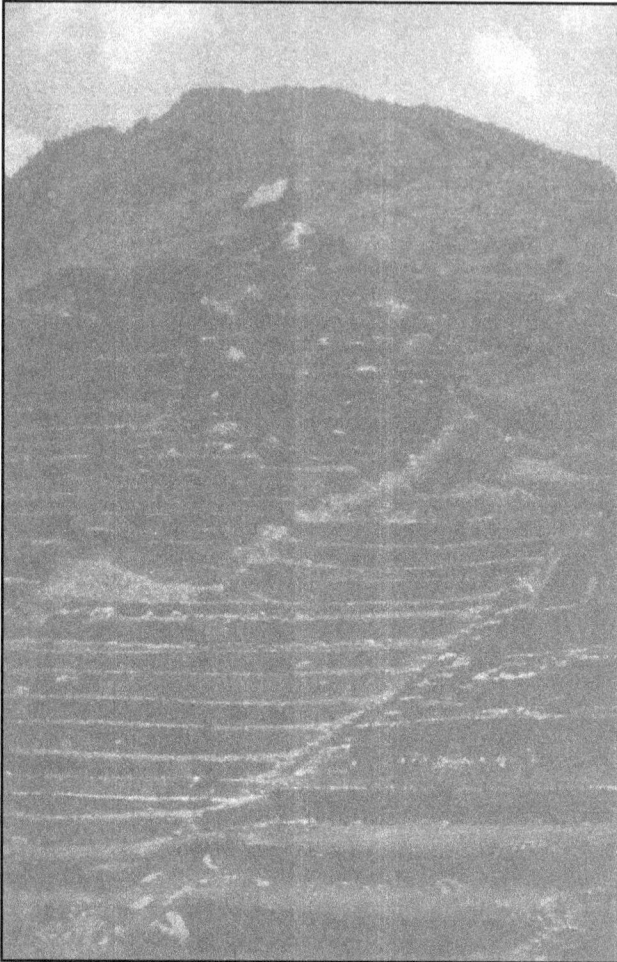

Five and a half acres of remarkable terraced walls and monuments still remain of thirteenth century Machu Picchu. Though many of their techniques of civilization appear to have been highly advanced, in particular their incomparable building skills, little is known of the people who lived here.

THE
GREENWICH
REVIEW

date unknown

A South American Journal

Rio de Janeiro was the final stop on a recent, two-week visit to South America made by John Winthrop of Greenwich while on leave from the chairmanship of Wood, Struthers & Winthrop Management Company in New York, prior to working for the George H. W. Bush campaign. The tour, though brief, encompassed Peru, with its ancient capital of the Incas; Argentina, the business center of today; and Brazil, promising land of tomorrow. Presented with permission in our prior issues have been glimpses of Peru and Argentina, and now, a look at Rio, from "A South American Journal."

The factory and display rooms of H. Stern, Brazil's and possibly the world's foremost jeweler, are a great attraction for visitors to Rio de Janeiro.

RIO DE JANEIRO, BRAZIL
November 8, 1979

Rio is hot in November – at least when the sun is out, it's hot. I awoke reasonably early on the morning of November 8. It was uncomfortably warm by nine o'clock. Over breakfast, I pondered the major points of interest in Peru and Argentina. In Peru, the Temple of the Sun and Machu Picchu; in Argentina, the Valdez Peninsula and Iguacu Falls were the highlights. In Rio, the gemstones and the beaches were to be the most indelible memories.

Immediately after breakfast, I was provided with a chauffeur-driven car by

H. Stem, the foremost jeweler in Brazil and, perhaps, the world. This courtesy ride to the factory, where the gems are cut and polished, is open to all the tourists in the top hotels who have an interest it seemed. I was driven to the heart of Rio – bypassing beaches along the way. Eventually, I was left outside a nondescript building and ushered up to the sixth floor. Presently, with a small group, I was shown along a corridor with walls of glass. Beyond the glass on one side, workers were working on individual rough stones – aquamarines, amethysts, topaz, tourmalines, beryls and many others. They were polishing and cutting these stones one by one, and with great care. We watched in fascination for fifteen minutes, then went down a circular staircase to the place where gems were displayed and sold.

On the floor below, individual salesmen sat at mahogany desks. Three chairs faced each one on the other side. A young girl, with hands folded in her lap, would sit by the side of the salesman. She would get stones or pour coffee upon request, and act as a messenger. A scribe or bookkeeper would appear on the scene as a third member of the team, as deals were closed. The whole process was intriguing. Never have I seen so many stones of value in a single room.

I presented my salesman with a letter I had been given to Mr. Stern. The next half hour, the salesman, Marc by name, educated me on what many have come to believe to be one of the better inflation hedges. At the end of the session, I told Marc I would return the next day and hoped to meet Mr. Stern. A car was waiting for me outside to take me back to the hotel.

As soon as I could get on a bathing suit, I was on the hot sands of the beach, running barefoot to get to the water's edge. All around me, beach boys and sea nymphs were cavorting on the sands – playing ball, walking, strolling arm in arm, or plunging into the big waves. All the bathing suits seemed very brief; all the people seemed to be enjoying themselves. It was a far happier place than the mountains of Peru.

The Rio night life is, of course, famous.

After the poverty-stricken mountain villages of Peru, opulent Rio with its international sophistication, luxurious shops and world famous beaches was a striking contrast.

From its site atop the Corcovado, the 125' figure of El Cristo dominates the city of Rio and its broad harbor, and is visible far out to sea. Spectacular lookouts dot the steep path to the summit.

One can select any type of night life that seems appealing. But, one is also aware of a large number of street urchins and prostitutes at night. This city is an odd combination of wealth and poverty, elegance and squalor.

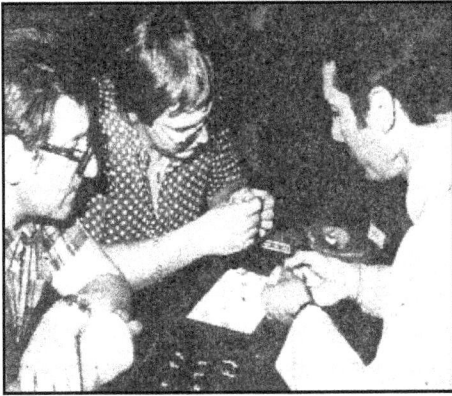

At H. Stern, after watching – through a glass wall – the actual cutting and polishing of the gems, visitors are led down to the show rooms for closer perusal and purchases.

The country dominates South America, and the people are very proud.

Brazil is going through an important transformation. One can almost feel it in the air and only hope that the fringes of poverty do not spread into a cancer.

November 9

Again the day began by a trip to the jewelry store, where I was able to pick up a gift or two. Mr. Stern was in the store and was nice enough to spend some time with me. He was particularly interested in what had happened at Tiffany in its merger with Avon. I told him all I knew and urged him not to follow in the footsteps of Mr. Hoving.

Lucky Roosevelt and Frank Shakespear (in Washington and Connecticut respectively), had urged me to meet Vivi Nabuco. She had been described as a beautiful woman, and that she is. She and her sister, Nininha, not only invited me for lunch, but also provided me with an air-conditioned limousine with a driver, for a trip up to the Christ statue on Corcovado. Luncheon began at approximately two,

and went on until four. A third lady joined us, and four of us ate by poolside. Three immaculately dressed man servants, in white tunics and black trousers, served unusual curried and salad delicacies, along with two wines and a coconut desert. It was another world! All of us joked about how spoiled I would be after such an experience, but it was an everyday occurrence on Rue Igatu, where the Nabuco sisters live.

I left with my driver to see El Cristo on the top of the mountain. Obviously, the view would be hopelessly obscured, as a heavy fog had set in, but I decided to go ahead anyway. The long climb up the mountainside proved worth it for, as I arrived at the summit, I found that I was the only human being at this high point of the city. There, above me, was the famous statue of Christ with arms outstretched, but almost obscured by fog. I took some pictures – my final ones in South America – as I looked above me at the splendid mass of stone. I had climbed two hundred nineteen steps – past a lovely variety of flowers and a couple of abandoned tourist stands to get to this spot. The solitude I felt could only remind me of a visit I had made to the Parthenon in Athens alone in a thunderstorm years before. It had been a very moving experience, as was this. Perhaps I felt too close to the hand of God, for I wasn't concentrating as I descended the stairs and slipped rather badly. The camera hit the marble steps and wouldn't work afterwards – a rather dramatic way to end my picture taking on this last day of my trip to South America!

1986

Touching the reality of the problems of Africa

John Winthrop, who lives in Greenwich recently spent a month in Africa with three of his sons. This is the first of three columns which will appear on consecutive days, commenting on his trip. This material is excerpted from a diary the author kept during his travel. The writer owns an investment firm in New York and is a former director of the National Audubon Society.

If you are among those who enjoy travel and if you believe that an investment in travel is worth as much or more than the expense of education in today's world, then you will be receptive to the idea that a trip to South Africa. Botswana and Zimbabwe this year was a good idea.

Others may be amused by a cousin who compared the trip with going to Berlin in 1943 or agree with my insurance man who called me an idiot.

Why Africa? While that continent is a study in contrasts and cultures and while one must be careful about generalizations when the subject arises. one can say with certainty that some of the human race's most conspicuous problems are etched in bold letters on that continent. Among them ...

Political – All over the world people have a difficult time understanding one another. The art of diplomacy and the need for people to communicate effectively with one another has never been more obvious than in today's world. If you want to see firsthand a country in the grips of political problems, you have to go to South Africa.

JOHN WINTHROP

Greenwich Time Board of Contributors

It is a country in agony today with intense feelings and crosscurrents, which are neither understood nor studied carefully by most Americans. We wanted to see it firsthand.

Environmental – Our planet is suffering degradation of our life support system in a dramatic way. We have been careless about defending wildlife and developing an environmental grand design for our grandchildren's existence. Where better can one see the most dramatic assemblage of big game and other wildlife than in Botswana, while at the same time, developing an understanding of what happens when heavy rains follow a five-yea r drought? We wanted to see it rather than read about it.

Economic – Some of the poorest nations in Africa are experiencing a four percent growth in population with no economic infrastructure, no market for produce and declining commodity prices.

The situation varies. of course, from country to country, but the classic economic pincher action leading toward economic chaos is unfolding in Africa. We wanted to develop greater sensitivity to that process.

Creative solutions to all of the above are not in evidence. We are moving with greater speed toward a more global economy. Hopefully, we will develop a greater awareness of our dwindling resources. Events push us toward the necessity of trying to understand each other better.

So for all of these reasons we planned a trip to the southern tip of the African continent. It was done with some urgency. Each of my three older boys (ages 17-22) left Greenwich to join me as well. As young adults they would provide some clarity of thought, some comic relief and they would provide their father with very good company on this once-in-a-lifetime trip.

On Bayard's Performance

On safari, as in life , Bayard is always performing, always holding center stage. "King Biscuit," as he is called, tells a lot about Bayard, but not all. He was quick to make new friends on this trip, quick to learn the techniques of bird hunting and quick to contribute mightily to the entertainment of the journey.

But Bayard has a great deal on his mind with the pressures of college and brothers and summer reading.

Sometimes it is understandably tempting to sit down and have a big meal in the dining tent and go to sleep in the afternoon.

Way down deep Bayard is a fighter and, a survivor, I suspect. My guess is that he will find his "place in the sun" without constant badgering from his father.

On Growing a beard

Growing a beard is almost like discovering a new and unfortunate side of one's personality. It starts out looking bad. After a few days it looks worse. Finally, it becomes frightening.

Incredulously, one's bearded face looks back in the reflection – a shadow on top of one's former self and yet part of the dark shadow is unexpectedly gray.

What a freak show! I had better take it off before I go home. While on safari is probably the best time to grow a beard.

On a new friend

We made friends with a man in Botswana named Berri. He is a man of middle age with a wonderful smiling face and with a real sense of pride in his work . Berri finds game and assists in the hunt.

Communication with this gentleman was difficult, and yet with the exchange of a few words I knew he had a sense of humor. that he appreciated beauty and that he had a real sense of' compassion as well.

No doubt across this vast continent there are many, many people with these qualities.

Sadly, there are not many smiles in Africa in the 1980s; the problems of politics. Of starvation, of economic disaster are simply too immense.

There were empty moments on safari when I wished I could do more for Berri. It was perhaps easiest to accept his friendship for what it was. Before leaving, Bayard gave him his safari hat. Clearly, this made him a happy man.

On Black Africa

The white man still seems to dominate the small slice of Africa we see. The black man is uneducated. He does the cooking, the laundry, the carrying, the hauling, the dog work. Worst of all, he often doesn't work at all. The unemployment rate is climbing to the sky and industrial development isn't coming fast enough to cure the problem.

The mindset of most white people toward the blacks seems somewhat different from ours, although a significant minority seem to show a compassion that is noteworthy. With sanctions it is clear from this vantage point in Botswana, which is so very dependent on South Africa that the blacks will only suffer more. Our brief stay in Johannesburg reinforced this viewpoint.

Perversely well-intentioned Europeans and Americans, who want to see the lot of the underdogs improved, only create a greater burden for the blacks. Sanctions can only swell the ranks of the unemployed throughout the southern part of this continent. Those whose lot we want to improve so badly appear to face something close to economic chaos as the population climbs. It is not a happy picture.

On Tribes

We passed the poor black people in the roads, by the rivers, in the towns. Always they waved; always they seemed friendly. But we had almost no idea of their culture or of their language.

Each of the over 5O countries in Africa – or at least most of them – have distinct differences among the different tribes of black people. One can devote a lifetime of study to understanding the various cultures and customs of the various tribes.

A dominant impression as we prepare to leave is that people everywhere – despite their differences and despite the difficulties in communication – seem friendly.

We went into a town named Seronga near a fishing camp in northwestern Botswana and found flocks of children coming out to stare at us and to wave enthusiastically.

Never have I seen greater joy in young faces anywhere.

The experience will remain with me for a long, long time. I don't know to this day of what tribe they were, but somehow it didn't make any difference.

1986

The fragile world of the wild animals of Africa

John Winthrop, who lives in Greenwich, recently spent a month in Africa with three of his sons. This is the second of three columns based on a diary the author kept during the trip. The writer owns an investment firm in New York and is a former director of the National Audubon Society.

On Green Monkeys

Green monkeys – playful fellows – skipping from tree to tree, green monkeys were the first animals we saw in Africa. They were curious and very athletic as they jumped from branch to branch trying to get a good look at the newcomers while we drove toward Mombo in central Botswana.

It was only after we were told about it that we could send these animals into a frenzy by jumping on the ground and chasing them or in showing our teeth – a sign of hostility. But upon reflection, why should anyone want to show hostility toward the green monkey or any other creature in big game country. Their world is a particularly fragile one.

On Lions

Sleepy, carnivorous, regal, lazy, elegant – so many words describe the lion. Yet nothing can adequately describe the unique thrill of happening upon a pride of lions as we did twice in Mombo deep inside Botswana.

The first time was at dusk. My son Gren sighted one large male with three

JOHN WINTHROP

Greenwich Time Board of Contributors

others under a thorn bush. We backed our vehicle up immediately to within yards of these splendid animals and began taking pictures.

Again, the next day in broad daylight, we sighted two on a road by the tall grass. One can sense that the encounter with a lion in the wilds is a very dramatic experience. Time almost stops as the shutters click, but, sadly, the magic can never quite be recorded on film.

Lions will always be star performers in big game country.

On Hippos

They say hippos don't congregate in big numbers anymore and generally they don't. But in Linyanti we traveled half a day to a large watering hole where we sighted between 40 and 50 of these heavy primeval beasts. Wallowing in a small pond, yawning in a vaguely threatening way, they almost ignored us even as we set up a picnic table to enjoy this extraordinary spectacle over lunch.

Off on one side of the pond a mother hippo nudged a dead calf with her big nose trying to bring him into the water with the others. She wouldn't leave it, somehow unwilling to accept the loss. This was a sad and even poignant side show to a main spectacle, which rivaled any seen by the early explorers more than a century ago.

That was a picnic lunch the four of us will remember.

On Elephants

Four enormous elephants surrounded a large tree on the edge of the road as we headed toward our camp in Linyanti. They were feeding on the branches and vines as they tore up the landscape with casual ruthlessness. Our car stopped so we could view them in action.

Only rarely did these elephants seem to notice us. It was almost as if their very size gave them total dominance over all other forms of life. We accepted this attitude happily. It was only when the car pushed on near one of the bulls that he turned toward us with ears flapping. Without trumpeting to the skies he merely took some dirt and blew it into the air. The territory belonged to him.

On Cows

Throughout Botswana and much of Africa cows are trying to survive on over-grazed land. Among black rural people they are the very symbol of wealth and prestige. Cows compete for habitat with the big game – a more important asset which attract tourists and safari trips.

The cattle provide scant return in meat or milk considering the expenditure of labor to provide for them. Burrows and natives haul water in big steel drums during the dry season so the cattle can drink.

A random view of any third world country makes us aware of the good fortune of the industrialized countries – at least in terms of the basic comforts of life.

On Doves

My son Jay mentioned that a dead dove held with wings outstretched and head drooping was a Christ symbol. It never had occurred to me. But in the back of that dusty van late in the day the bird of peace looked particularly beautiful. The symbolism seemed powerfully valid.

On Ducks

Ducks are elegant and beautiful birds all over the world. They tear over the water at sunrise, darting like fighter planes, then floating like gliders. Poetry in space. I always think of ducks in the cold morning, but it gets warm early in Botswana.

The speed and the grace of ducks – no matter what their species – has always thrown a bolt of excitement into this fifty-year-old man and I guess they always will.

On Guinea Fowl

A guinea is an ugly bird with a spotted fat body and a head like a vulture. As a bird to hunt, however, they provide drama and excitement.

Guinea fowl are fast runners. They congregate frequently in large numbers from 20 to 50. They take off slowly but build up a good speed and then glide over the tree tops.

If well placed, the hunters get a shot at these creatures as the beaters herd them and get them into the air with loud cries.

The guinea fowl of Africa provides the upland game hunter with a great deal of excitement and a good meal if he gets a square hit.

April 2005

A Trip Through the Panama Canal:
January 26 – February 5, 2005

The history, the sacrifice and the drama involved in constructing the Panama Canal are described in detail in a wonderful book, "The Path Between the Seas," by David McCullough. That gifted speaker and Pulitzer prize-winning author joined a small group of us on a Crystal Cruise line voyage to the Canal. My wife and I were sent an invitation by the Massachusetts Historical Society to join a small group. We accepted. David McCullough must be given credit for most of the words that follow. He added new dimensions to the experience.

Climbing into a cloudless sky, we took a Delta flight directly to Fort Lauderdale from Charleston, S, C. The next day we boarded the cruise ship Crystal Harmony. With its responsive and professional staff of more than five hundred and its reputation for superb food, we knew this was not going to be a hardship cruise for any of us.

After several days at sea with brief visits to St Thomas, St. Marteen, St. Bart's and Aruba, we were treated by David McCullough to a pair of formal lectures and many informal meetings – often while consuming banquet-style feasts. In the process we learned much about the saga and the history of the building of the Canal.

Some of the well-known and less well-known facts about the Canal and about Panama can be listed...

- It is clearly one of the busiest sea lanes in the world, The full length is roughly fifty miles.
- It runs from northwest to southeast going toward the Pacific.
- The Canal entrance is roughly due south of Pittsburgh, Pa. – further east than most realize.
- The lowest toll for passage (based on total tonnage) was thirty-six cents (a swim by the famed adventurer, Richard Haliburton). Our ship paid a toll of $115, 000!
- It is not a cut between the seas but rather a man made lake carved in the mountains with locks on either side.

The country of Panama – approximately the size of South Carolina – has a greater variety of birdlife than all of North America.

The Panama Canal was started by the French in 1879. They deserve far more credit than is generally realized, despite mistakes in judgment; despite evidence of bribery and corruption; and despite the eventual failure and bankruptcy of the enterprise.

The work was completed by the United States – largely as a result of the inspiring leadership of President Teddy Roosevelt who visited the Canal while work was underway – thus becoming the first President to venture outside of the United States while in office. The first ship sailed through the Canal on August 3, 1914. On that date work had been completed under budget, ahead of time, and without a trace of corruption.

By any measure the building of the Canal was a remarkable achievement. Workers from ninety countries participated in the effort. Most of them were black laborers – working under terrible conditions with midday temperatures rising to well over 100 degrees. Malaria and yellow fever claimed most of the twenty-five thousand lives lost in the undertaking (amounting to about five hundred deaths per mile!) It was the work of Dr. Gorges, who virtually eliminated the diseases that made the medical advances as consequential, if not more so, than the more obvious engineering achievement.

While the eventual costs of the enterprise measure about six hundred million dollars, or far less than the "Big Dig" in current dollars, the benefits of the Panama Canal have been immeasurable. The savings in ocean travel from New York to San Francisco, alone, is about eight thousand miles!

It must be added that the Canal project was initiated and undertaken for very positive reasons and with great excitement by everyone involved. Ironically it was completed as World War I began – thus ending the ideological mindset on the beginning of the last century. Nevertheless, as David McCullough pointed out, it was the equivalent of the moon landing of its time. His book must be read to fully appreciate the wonder and the drama of the story.

As we approached the Canal before sunrise, we could see a number of other ships awaiting their turn for passage through the locks. The waning moon was clearly visible above us. The sea was relatively calm. A cool breeze drifted across the bow where we stood. As we approached the Gatun Locks, we noticed a small inlet – a ditch – marking the spot where the French began their doomed effort. It was not marked or highlighted in any way.

Gradually the rising sun peeked through scattered clouds to our left. Native frigate birds floated by over head; some pelicans rested on the water. The dense, green, lush jungle lay on all sides – the source of all the water flowing from the Chagres River makes the Panama Canal work. The man made Gatun Lake (the largest ever created) formed the "bridge" far ahead of us allowing all the vessels to pass across the lake and through the locks.

Entering the locks, we were struck by the silence of the world surrounding us and also of the enormous size of the locks themselves – nearly the size of the Chrysler Building lying down, we were told. While trying to absorb all of this, with human beings and cars on land seemingly dwarfed by their surroundings, water was effortlessly lifting our eighty-ton vessel. The endless expanse of jungle off to our right showed no billboards or signs of urban sprawl. It was very, very peaceful and inspiring.

Beside the locks we saw the hydroelectric dam which supplied the energy for the entire enterprise – allowing us to fully appreciate the perpetual motion machine that allowed "the canal to function, for over ninety years. In addition to the scenery, we were reminded of the extraordinary result of coupling man's entrepreneurial genius with the force of nature as opposed to the alternative idea of simply digging a ditch between the oceans, which would have denied the force of the river, thus working against nature and would have been "mission impossible". Working with nature allowed the dream to materialize!

Needless to say the trip provided us with a lifelong memory. The pictures we took and the words used to describe the experience simply are not adequate. It can be said, however, that the experience provides the traveler with a renewed sense of wonder concerning the beauty of our planet as well and the genius and the sacrifice and the diversity of the people who created the Panama Canal over ninety years ago. We stand on the shoulders of all those who have gone before us.

The Hampton
County Guardian

Wednesday, September 8, 1982

Farewell to Frances White

Last week we lost a friend. Over four generations the Winthrop family has learned something about the wonderful qualities that made Frances White the exceptional person she was. She had a rare warmth and kindness. We never knew her to speak ill of others. As a midwife she brought many, many people into this world; as a nurse she cared for the sick and the young; as a human being she gave us brightness and good cheer and a splendid, rich, uplifting sense of humor.

Without shame she talked of God. She drew strength from Him. In all these ways she gave us inspiration. Now that Frances White is no longer with us members of the Winthrop family know that she gave all of us far, far more than we gave her. We shall miss her terribly, but know that she has found peace now. We only wish we could have been here to say good-by.

JOHN WINTHROP
AUGUST, 1982